ANCHORING
All techniques for all bottoms

ANCHORING

All techniques for all bottoms

by

DON BAMFORD

Drawings by Michael Blaser

SEVEN SEAS PRESS, INC. NEWPORT, RI 02840

Published by Seven Seas Press, Inc., Newport, Rhode Island 02840

Copyright © 1985 by D. A. Bamford
Illustrations Copyright © 1985 by Michael Blaser

Library of Congress Cataloging in Publication Data

Bamford, Don, 1930–
Anchoring.

Includes index.
1. Mooring of ships.   2. Anchorage.   3. Boats and
boating—Safety measures.   I. Title.
VK545.B36   1985   623.8′62   84-13935
ISBN 0-915160-64-1

1 3 5 7 9 RR/RR 0 8 6 4 2

Designed by Irving Perkins Associates
Printed in the United States of America by R. R. Donnelley & Sons
Edited by James R. Gilbert
Technical editing by Dale Nouse

Dedicated to Jean, my first mate for forty-two years.

She has put up with much, including the disproportionate attention I lavish on my mistress.

She has shared many adventures, while not always sharing my addiction to sailing.

She has tolerated patiently the hours, even months I have spent studying and writing.

Jean continues to sail and cruise distant waters as first mate.

ACKNOWLEDGMENTS

I must acknowledge that the bulk of the information contained here did not derive from my own personal experience.

I am indebted to all those fellow sailors who have written so well about their experiences with anchors and other ground tackle in the ultimate testing grounds. Among them are my friends Lin and Larry Pardey, Hal Roth, Miles Smeeton and Don Street. Their expertise, and that of a great many others, is boiled down, and I hope interpreted correctly, into this work.

I am indebted, also, to the many manufacturers of ground tackle who have supplied information. In particular I welcomed help from L.C.D.R. USNR (ret.) Robert Danforth Ogg, now retired from the Danforth Co., who answered my questions and passed on his thoughts on the subject quite frankly. A further word of thanks goes to John Charters of Bellevue, Quebec who introduced me to the French tests described in the text.

There are very few books on the subject. Those which have been most helpful for reference are: *Chapman: Piloting, Seamanship and Small Boat Handling* by Elbert S. Maloney (The Hearst Corp.); *Anchors & Anchoring* by R. D. Ogg (The Danforth Co.); *Anchor Selection & Use* by Robert A. Smith; *Oceanography & Seamanship* by William A. Van Dorn (Dodd, Mead & Co., Inc.).

CONTENTS

CONTENTS

viii

INTRODUCTION

Anchors have been symbols of security since the beginning of water transportation and have been mentioned in the literature from the times of the early Greeks.

Despite the wisdom passed on by very experienced cruising people over the years, the fitting out with proper ground tackle and the skill in using it properly probably is the most abused and neglected facet of pleasure-boat seamanship. Beyond doubt, it is one of the principal reasons for loss or damage to yachts.

It frequently is said that you can tell the caliber of a seaman by a glance at his ground tackle. If this statement is correct, less than one in 10 of those who tie up at marinas have learned their lesson. Anchors are rarely seen at all (and most anchor lockers on deck are too small for suitable gear). Undoubtedly many feel they will spend their sailing time making short hops from one marina to the next and, as long as they do, they may never need an anchor.

Life and boating are at their best unpredictable. You don't buy anchors—or any kind of insurance—because you expect catastrophe, but because you know it exists.

Bill Rogan and his wife were not inexperienced sailors. On June 9, 1983, they were bringing their newly acquired Alberg 37 from Sarnia to Bayfield on Lake Huron, with their two children as crew.

It was a bright, calm, sunny day and all was well with the world. Winds were too light to sail so the yacht was under power. At 11:30 a.m. the engine stopped and Bill tried vainly for hours to restart it.

Around two p.m., a breeze came up straight from their intended course and they were unable to make much headway towards port. The winds gradually increased and at nine p.m. Bill arranged by radio for a marine mechanic to be brought out by the police. So far there was no danger, merely discomfort and increasing anxiety. Despite all efforts, the engine could not be started. By 11:30 the waves were estimated at 10 to 12' high, the winds at 40 knots. Adding to the family's troubles, both the mechanic and one of the children were seasick.

The Coast Guard suggested Bill anchor and they would take off the crew. At this time they were about ¾ of a mile from a lee shore in some 35' of water with a hard sand bottom.

Bill set a 33 lb. Bruce anchor with 60' of ⁵⁄₁₆" chain and 200' of ¾" nylon rode. The Coast Guard thought it unwise to use a cutter in such conditions and so a helicopter removed all five, setting them down on the beach nearby.

Twelve hours later, the wind and waves had subsided to the point where Bill was taken back to *Watooka* and the trip continued. No damage was suffered.

The lesson here is that even the most experienced of cruising people can get into trouble when they neglect proper anchoring techniques. That lesson, if ever it required underscoring, was made painfully clear to the sailing world on a beautiful, balmy December day in 1982. Close to 50 yachts had gathered from near and far and were anchored in the anchorage at Cabo San Lucas, Mexico.

A squall hit the anchorage in early evening. It turned into a screaming gale lasting most of the night with winds over 50 knots whipping up 20′ surf.

In all, 27 boats went ashore with anchors dragged or rodes parted. Of these, 21 were damaged severely, most beyond repair. Only six were salvaged to sail again. An even dozen boats managed to sail out into the ocean where they weathered the storm with no damage. Several yachts sank or disappeared where they were anchored. A few moved to safety in the inner harbor. In all, only six boats held safely on their anchors and escaped with little or no damage.

Even the world-famous sailor Bernard Moitessier lost his beloved yacht *Joshua* in the catastrophe, though it later was salvaged by a new owner.

Most of the yachts had adequate ground tackle but were deficient in their techniques. Others fell prey to a weak link somewhere in their systems. Nearly all, including Moitessier, misread the weather signs and were guilty of anchoring much too close to shore. (We'll look at this incident again in our discussion of techniques for much can be learned from the failures of others.)

Good seamanship does pay off. In August of 1980, Hurrican Doreen hit the small harbor of Escondido, some 250 miles north of Cabo San Lucas. Twelve yachts were in harbor. All those with crew on board were able to set proper anchors. They all survived more than 24 hours of gale-force winds, gusting to 75 knots at times.

Fortunately, anchors rarely are needed 'in extremis.' Cruising families will spend hundreds of pleasant nights in remote anchorages and only rarely is the ground tackle severely strained. The knowledge that we are securely attached to the bottom helps us sleep in peace, an essential aspect of happy cruising.

Similarly, knowing how to handle your boat efficiently in and around docks, and being able to secure it exactly where you want it, not only is good seamanship, but it's the best protection against yard bills and insurance claims. Almost all the bruises and scratches your hull endures occur in and around docks.

Also, the little mistakes you make in open water generally are inconsequential and often unseen. In an occupied anchorage or a busy marina, you are on stage. Everyone is watching your performance with a critical eye, judging your capabilities. Are you giving a lubberly or seamanlike performance?

Anchoring, docking and mooring are all part of the seaman's art. As in all art, no one ever reaches perfection. The best sailors invariably are those who never stop learning. Always there exists a new and better piece of gear, a safer and easier technique.

It is my hope the knowledge imparted in this book, gleaned from years of personal experience and from the accounts of hundreds of others, will help every reader enjoy safer, more carefree boating. You may never win a public accolade for your docking and anchoring performances, but I promise you won't be marked down as a lubberly neophyte either.

ANCHORING
All techniques for all bottoms

CHAPTER 1

Defining The Terms

I am a bit of a nut on the proper use of nautical terms ever since a boat show salesman tried to convince me that "cabin sole" was the same thing as private cabin. You may already know what all the principal words mean, but it never hurts to learn a few more. It actually matters little what definition one uses, as long as proper practice is observed. But following this book will be simplified if readers know how I prefer to use various nautical terms. Not only will we all be talking the same language, but I won't have to interrupt later discussions to explain key words and terms.

It must be pointed out that in this subject there is frequent disagreement on the use and definition of words. Take "scope." Chapman describes it as the ratio of rode length to water depth. Des Sleightholme, the editor of *Yachting Monthly,* uses the same meaning. *The Encyclopedia of Sailing,* however, defines scope as the length of mooring or anchor line in use. These are important differences in meaning.

Similarly, some authors use "kedge" as another name for a fisherman anchor, while others refer to it as a smaller anchor used to move a boat from one place to another.

And again, while none of my dictionaries permit the usage, several English authors use the word "warp" in reference to mooring lines.

I will not be dogmatic about proper definitions and insist that the definitions here are the only correct ones. To the best of my knowledge and research, they are the ones in most common use among English-speaking sailors, though there are several whose meanings differ between the U.K. and America.

I have grouped the words under a few general headings. Hopefully, this will make them easier to find.

ANCHORS AND THEIR PARTS

An anchor is a specially shaped device designed to bury efficiently into the bottom and hold the vessel in place. Alternatively, an anchor may be designed to hook onto coral or rock or other bottom material.

A *bower anchor* is any anchor stored at the bows, ready for use. The *best bower* is a working anchor, not necessarily the heaviest. It usually is carried to port in the Northern Hemisphere to ensure an open hawse, then it is referred to as the *port bower*. Similarly the *starboard bower*.

The *storm anchor* is your heaviest anchor, always set when expecting the worst of conditions. It should be set, also, when you are leaving the boat at anchor for a time and not certain what may happen while you are away. The term *sheet anchor* means the same thing. It is synonymous with "security."

A *breast anchor* is set off the side of the boat, usually to hold it away from a dock or berth.

A *stern anchor*, sometimes called a *stream anchor*, is set off the stern.

Principal parts of various anchors.

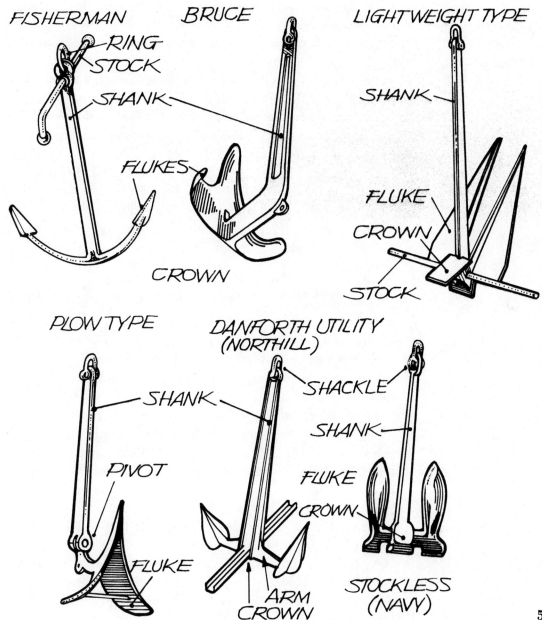

FISHERMAN

BRUCE

LIGHTWEIGHT TYPE

RING

STOCK

SHANK

FLUKES

CROWN

SHANK

FLUKE

CROWN

STOCK

PLOW TYPE

DANFORTH UTILITY (NORTHILL)

SHANK

PIVOT

FLUKE

SHACKLE

SHANK

FLUKE

CROWN

ARM

CROWN

STOCKLESS (NAVY)

5

The *kedge* is the largest anchor on board which is not too large to be carried in your dinghy. It is primarily intended for kedging off a grounding or for moving the boat from one place to another.

The *shank* is the part joining the crown and/or stock to the ring.

The *stock* is the part that lies at right angles to the shank, sometimes at the crown, sometimes near the ring.

The *crown* is the end of the shank opposite the ring, where the stock crosses the shank if there is one. It's the point of pivot of the plow.

The *fluke* is the large flat area, also called the *palm* and usually pointed at the leading edge, which is called the *bill*. The words palm and bill are rarely used today.

The *ring* is the place where the rode is attached. Frequently it is a steel ring.

ANCHORING PROCEDURES AND TECHNIQUES

A vessel in coastal waters is said to be *on soundings*. When she is well offshore she is *off soundings*. For our purposes here, we will consider "on soundings" to imply that the vessel is in depths where it is possible to anchor, which may, at times, be several hundred feet.

To *sound* or *take soundings* is to measure the depth below the yacht, most frequently done today with an electronic echo-sounder. It also can be done with a sounding line and lead. The lead is *armed* by putting tallow in the depression in the bottom, so that some of the bottom material will stick to it.

An anchor is *dropped* or *lowered*. It is never thrown out, cast or heaved.

As the boat backs down the anchor will start to *hook*, or catch on the bottom. As the boat backs down harder, it will *dig in* and eventually *bury*. This burying is referred to as *setting* the anchor.

Once anchored, an *anchor watch* frequently is established. A crewmember may be delegated to watch for dragging, chafe and other hazards.

A vessel using a long scope is referred to as lying to a *long stay*. When the vessel is in the act of *weighing*, i.e., raising the anchor and leaving, it comes to a *short stay*. As it comes over the anchor, the rode is *up and down*, then it *breaks out* and is raised to the bow or chock. If hanging from the bow roller, ready to lower, it is *a-cock-bill*.

Sometimes, in lieu of *break out* the expression *trip* the anchor is used. This is more accurately employed when the anchor is hauled out backwards with a *trip line*, normally attached to its crown.

Sometimes an anchor *breaks out* accidentally, i.e., releases its hold on the bottom, causing it to *drag*.

At times, however, an anchor is deliberately dragged across the harbor, and used to control the movement of the boat in a stream or tideway. This operation is called *drudging*.

Kedging is moving a boat by hauling on a line (or cable or warp) attached to an anchor, well dug in some distance away.

An anchor is said to be *becued* when its rode is secured to the crown instead of the ring. The rode then is seized to the ring with light line, so that if the anchor fouls, the seizing will snap, allowing the anchor to be tripped.

LASHING OF LIGHT LINE

An anchor becued with rode shackled to the crown and tied with light line to the crown.

7

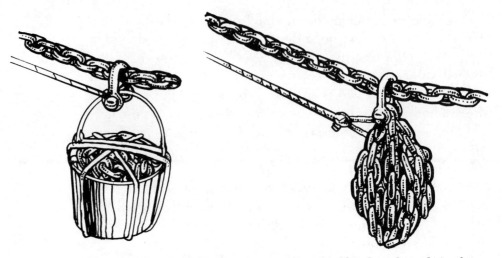

Two possible riding weights. Do not use a shackle when the rode is of rope as it may abrade the rode.

An anchor cable *grows* indicating the direction in which the cable is running from the bow.

If two or more anchors are used, and the rodes become crossed, they are referred to as *foul hawse. Backing the anchor* is using a weight on the rode primarily to improve the *catenary* and thereby the shock-absorbing effect of the rode. It usually consists of sliding a weight down the rode using a large shackle or *traveller.* It may also be accomplished by tying part of the chain into a bundle and attaching it to the rode before lowering. The weight is called many names, *riding weight, chum, messenger, sentinel,* or *kellett.* (Not to be confused with *killick,* which is an old British term for small anchor or slang for anchor.)

LINES AND LINE HANDLING

Using the word *rope* generally is correct only while the material is on a spool or coil and not assigned to a specific purpose. Once assigned, it becomes a line, halyard, sheet, rode, warp or whatever.

8

The word *rode* comes from the old English word "road" meaning anchorage, also called "roadstead." It still is used at time, for example, Hampton Roads. In our context, rode is the *line* used for anchoring. In this book we will use rode to include the rope, chain or wire—or combination of these—and all shackles, swivels, etc.

On larger boats, one might refer to rode as *cable*. Some refer to the "anchor warp," which is not usually correct usage. The noun *warp* is a rope by which a vessel is moved about when in harbor. Therefore it is correct to refer to a *kedge warp* for a kedge is used for moving the boat. Similarly, the verb *warp* means the act of moving the vessel by means of a rope secured to a kedge, or a bollard or something else ashore.

Line is a general term used for ropes and cords used for various purposes on a vessel.

A *bridle* is a span of chain or rope with both ends secured and the strain taken in the middle.

An *anchor spring* or *anchor bridle* is a line secured, part way down the rode and led to a chock in the quarter or stern. By adjusting the tension between it and the rode the vessel's head may be swung for any reason, including to reduce rolling. The waves in an anchorage frequently do not roll at right angles to the breeze.

A *hockle* is a short tight bend or kink in a rope that has been twisted too hard or drawn too hastily off a coil. It's something to be avoided.

A hockle in a line will weaken it severely.

9

A chain-rope splice.

A *splice* is a method of joining two ropes or a rope and chain by interlacing the strands.

To *bend* is to fasten one rope to another or to some other object. A knot used to make this connection is the *anchor bend*, also known as the *fisherman's bend*.

To coil a rope on deck (or in a locker) in large circles or figure-of-eight turns so that it will run out freely is to *fake* or *flake* a rope. A chain is *ranged* out on deck for the same purpose.

Chafe is wear on a line, chain or wire due to rubbing against some sharp or rough object. *Chafe guard* is material wrapped around the line to prevent chafe. *Freshen the nip* is to change the location of any rope (by letting out or hauling in) so that chafe is not concentrated at one spot but spread over a fresh part of the line. *Freshen the hawse* refers to the same procedure. *End for end* is reversing the ends of a rope or chain to get more use from it or to reduce chafing. A *snubber* is a shock-absorbing device attached to a line to reduce the sudden strains. It can be of rubber, nylon, spring—even an old auto tire will do.

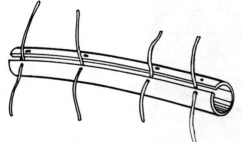

A purpose made chafe guard. You buy it in lengths of about 2 feet and cut it to size.

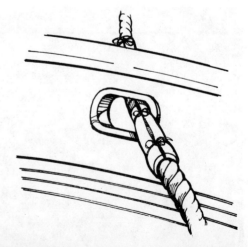

A strong, rubber snubber seen on a French yacht.

As an anchored vessel swings to wind or tide it is said to be *wind rode* or *tide rode* respectively.

Scope may be expressed as the length of rode in use from anchor to bow, e.g., 100 feet. Also it may be specified as the ratio of the length of rode in use, to the vertical distance from the bow to the bottom. Thirty-five feet of rode in 5′ of water is expressed as a 7:1 scope. It is desirable to think in terms of *scope ratio* for this has a great deal to do with the holding power of the anchor system under given conditions.

Catenary is the curve of chain or rope hanging between two points, e.g., between bow roller and bottom.

Chain is the steel counterpart of rope. It is supplied in *shots* or *shackles* usually 15 fathoms in length.

To *seize* a line is to lash it tightly with light line, e.g., to prevent the end from unravelling. It also is used to secure shackle pins, or when it is necessary to secure two pieces of rope together.

SEIZINGS

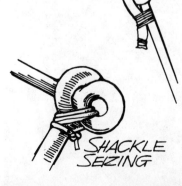

SHACKLE SEIZING

BOTTLE SCREW

CLOVE HITCH

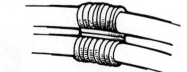

RACKING SEIZING

Lashing across a hook, making it more secure, is called "mousing".

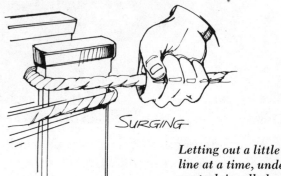

Letting out a little line at a time, under control, is called "surging" the line.

To *mouse* a hook is to lash across the opening with light line to prevent it from coming undone.

To *surge* a line is to let it out a little at a time, maintaining firm control.

Possibly the broadest term in anchoring is *ground tackle*, a general term that includes anchors, cables (rope, chain and wire), shackles, chocks, cleats or bitts, windlass, mooring lines, fenders, etc.

While not properly part of ground tackle, we also will consider in this book anchor lights and signals, snorkels and Scuba, dinghies and other such gear used in conjunction with anchoring.

DECK GEAR

Bitts were fitted on sailing ships in the early days. They were strong wooden or metal uprights to which the anchor rode

This finely fitted yacht sports a strong pair of bitts alongside the base of the bowsprit.

Heavy stainless steel bollards on a large, luxury power cruiser.

could be secured. They have been replaced by cleats, small bollards and/or Samson posts. From this word comes the term "bitter end," the end of a line or cable behind the bitts and made fast in the chain locker.

Bollards are usually heavy wood or metal heads set into a seawall or pier for securing or warping large ships. Smaller versions of these are sometimes found on metal yachts. They also are fabricated into some windlasses.

Bow roller is a device over which the anchor rope or chain rolls freely. Sometimes they also are designed to stow the anchor(s). Similar devices are often fitted to the bowsprit, rather than to the bow.

A well-faired opening in the bulwark of a vessel through which the hawser (for mooring) or anchor rode passes is called a *hawse hole*. A *hawse pipe* is a pipe in the topsides into which the shank of an anchor may be drawn. On yachts, a *chock* serves the same purpose. It is attached to or forms part of the toerail and usually is fitted at each side of the bow and at each quarter. They are particularly useful if fitted amidships as well.

A *cleat* is a fitting to which a line may be secured conveniently. Serving the same function are *Samson posts*, very strong posts fitted through the deck to the keel and used to

13

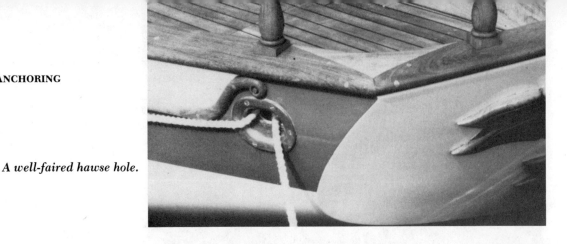

A well-faired hawse hole.

take the strain of the anchor line. They also are used for securing mooring lines or towing hawser and sometimes are fitted at the stern.

A device, usually permanently fitted in place, and used to take the strain of the chain off the windlass is a *chain stopper*. A *chain hook* attached to a piece of line is frequently used as a snubber with chain rodes. There are specially made hooks for this purpose called *devil's claw* or *chain claw*.

Cat-head is a term leftover from old sailing days. It is a support protruding to each side of the foredeck to which the anchor is hauled up in preparation for a voyage.

A tackle for lifting a heavy anchor aboard is a *burton*. We still speak of securing an anchor for sea as *catting the anchor*.

A deck fitting through which the chain or rope passes into the locker is a *navel* and sometimes is called a *deck pipe*.

Chock and cleat with rubber hose to prevent chafe.

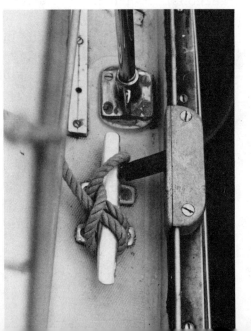

A Samson post, attached directly to the keel, makes a very strong point of attachment for anchor rode or mooring lines.

Usually a navel is incorporated into the design of a windlass or capstan.

A *windlass* is a mechanism for controlling an anchor rode as it is let out or hauled in. It has a horizontal shaft and usually is fitted with a drum around which a few turns of line may be wound, and a narrow, cast sheave specially fitted to take the chain. The line drum is called a *gypsy* (or *gipsy*) and the chain sheave, a *wildcat.* On some models the chain sheave also can handle rope. Usually a *stripper* is fitted to help remove the chain or rope, and to prevent it jamming at the navel.

A *capstan* essentially is the same as a windlass, though the shaft is vertical instead of horizontal. Some manufacturers call their capstans "vertical windlasses."

ANCHORAGES AND BOAT ACTIONS

When the boat does not have sufficient room to swing without danger of encountering hazards or other boats, it is said to have a *foul berth*.

Foul bottom is when the bottom is littered with debris, old chains, rocks, wrecks, logs or old mooring cables, which may prevent the anchor from holding, or make it difficult to break out the anchor or weigh. *Foul anchor* is when the rode is tangled with a fluke or crown, or when it is caught in debris, coral, rocks, etc., and cannot be broken out.

When the bottom has been plowed up extensively by anchors dragging or even being broken out, leaving the bottom

15

Fisherman anchor fouled by rode.

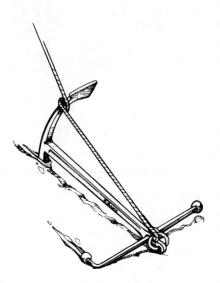

soft and not reliable holding, it is *scoured*. The bottom can also be scoured by current or a storm, leaving it loose and poor for holding.

A vessel is said to *swing* at anchor when it turns with change of wind or tide or other current. A vessel that does not lie steadily to her anchor but ranges from side to side is said to *sheer* about. The words *range* and sheer are used interchangeably to describe this action, also called *sailing about the anchor*.

In rough weather a vessel is described as *surging, pitching, heaving, bucking* and *plunging,* all of which are descriptive of the actions of the boat. Damage to anchor gear, destruction of china and much more down below, and disastrous effects on the crew's stomach and appetite may result very quickly. You will have your own very expressive words for this action as well!

The distance over which wind blows to form waves is called the *fetch*.

A change in water depth caused by differences in atmospheric pressure is called *seche*. Seches are common on the Great Lakes and can cause variations in depth as great as 7', though rarely more than a couple of feet. The phenomenon may develop quickly or slowly and may even appear as a wave.

A vessel, whether ship or yacht, does not back up, as does a land vehicle. She *backs down* or *makes sternway* or *goes astern.*

When it is desirable to take some strain off the mooring cable or anchor rode in a storm by powering into the wind and waves, this action is termed *dodging.*

Steerage way is the forward movement of the boat, which makes her able to answer to the helm and thus capable of control. A vessel that is *dead in the water* is at a standstill, though possibly drifting.

MOORING AND DOCKING

Words have an inconvenient habit of changing meaning with time and place.

In marine parlance, a *dock* is a basin into which a vessel is brought for loading, unloading or embarking and debarking passengers. In shore language it includes the *pier* or *wharf,* even the *quay.*

Hence we "dock" our boats in the water alongside a *finger pier,* for example, and we *secure alongside* or *make fast.* We never "tie up" the boat. That is a very lubberly expression. Or we may say, we *moor alongside* the pier.

We may secure to a *mooring* in a harbor. The mooring may be a mushroom anchor or heavy weight, or chains across the harbor bottom. Or it may be two or more anchors. The mooring, whatever it is on the bottom, typically is attached using chains to a *mooring buoy* on the surface. Note that a boat attached to two anchors is termed moored but not if the two anchors are in tandem.

We commonly use the words to *berth* or to *dock* interchangeably (not with precise accuracy) as verbs indicating the act of bringing our boats into a dock and securing along-

Typical mooring using mushroom anchor.

CHAFING GEAR
FLOAT
SHACKLE
LIGHT CHAIN
HEAVY CHAIN
ANCHOR

side. A vessel also is at its berth when attached to its assigned mooring buoy.

The vessel is secured with *mooring lines,* though on larger vessels they sometimes are called hawsers. There are three groups of mooring lines. *Breast lines* are normally run at approximately 90° to the fore-and-aft line of the vessel. A *spring line* runs at a sharp angle to the fore-and-aft line of the vessel and is used to limit movement fore and aft. A line from the bow forward is, typically, called the *bow line.* Similarly the line leading from the stern aft to the dock is the *stern line.*

Sometimes a line from the yacht is taken around a bollard and brought back to the yacht. It is referred to as *doubled*

A boat well-secured alongside. (1) Bowline, (2) Forward breast line, (3) Forward spring line, (4) Aft spring, (5) Aft breast, and (6) Stern line. In tidal waters, make allowance for change in water level. Breast lines may not be practical under tidal conditions.

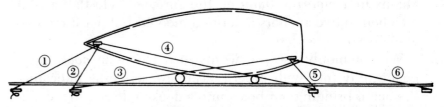

back. When two lines are taken from the yacht to the bollard, e.g., two bow lines, that is referred to as *doubling the lines.*

The vessel is kept away from the dock with *fenders* which, typically, are air-filled balloons of some plastic, or are of cork, or even rubber tires. Calling these "bumpers" is incorrect and lubberly.

When securing alongside a very irregular pier, or to pilings, a board frequently is attached to the outside of the fenders and is called a *fenderboard.*

It may be desirable, even essential, to protect the lines with *anti-chafe* material at the chocks and even at the pier—in fact anywhere they can rub and be abraded.

Frequently *snubbers,* usually of rubber, are fitted into the mooring lines to take any sudden shock as the vessel surges

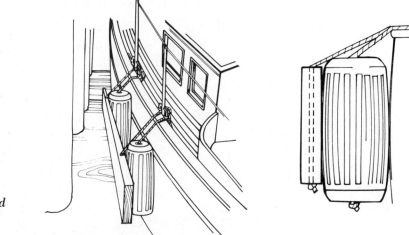

Typical fenderboard arrangement.

19

with waves. Snubbers may make the boat lie easier and reduce strain on the lines, thereby reducing abrasion at chocks and prolonging the life of the lines.

ORDERS, INSTRUCTIONS AND CREW ACTIONS

When making ready to leave your slip, the skipper (let's assume here the skipper is a man) may assign his well-trained crew to the appropriate positions on deck and issue these instructions.

Stand by the lines.

Single up all lines. Where lines are doubled, all but one is to be removed.

Cast off bow line, or cast off forward, or whichever line he refers to. Then he may say *handsomely.* It means smoothly, carefully, slowly.

Similarly, approaching your slip, he might order *get a line over* or *heave a line ashore.* Which line has been pre-arranged, usually a midship line.

Then he will *spring her in,* taking slight strain on the spring line and bringing the boat alongside in preparation to securing her.

He will order *secure the lines* and the crew will take the various spring lines and breast lines, bow and stern lines ashore and *make them fast*.

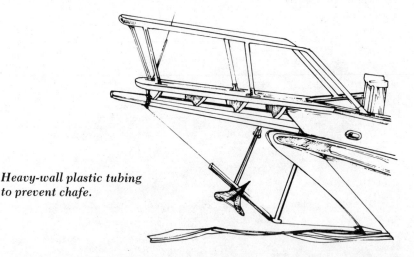

Heavy-wall plastic tubing to prevent chafe.

On approaching an anchorage, the orders might be *at the ready,* meaning get the anchor over and ready to lower.

Let go, lower away both mean the same thing: Lower the anchor. When the foredeck crew indicates the anchor is on bottom, the boat will continue to fall back or back down until the crew has *veered* or *payed out* adequate rode. Then the skipper will order *snub her there.* To snub a line is to suddenly stop its run, by taking extra turns, adding pressure, or by applying the windlass brake.

When he is satisfied that the anchor has started to dig in adequately, he may order, *veer more rode,* as he backs down further. When he has enough out, he may signal to *belay,* which is to *check* or stop the cable running. Again, *make fast* means to secure the cable either to bitts, cleat or by the windlass.

As the skipper powers up toward the anchor, getting ready to *weigh anchor,* the crew will *heave in* the rode. This does not mean throw it but rather pull it in, manually or by means of the windlass. The skipper may indicate *avast heaving* when he wants the crew to cease. He may order *heave taut,* which means to haul in the cable and take the strain.

When the crew has heaved sufficiently for the moment, he may call out *so!* which means stop pulling.

He may ask for the cable to be *belayed,* i.e., made fast, so he can break out the anchor by powering over it.

In emergency, the skipper may order the anchor to be *slipped.* In this case, a fender or float is attached to the rode and is dropped over the side. Hopefully, you can return at a later time to retrieve the anchor.

The word *ease* means to gently slacken off a line.

The word *surge* means to slacken a line or cable suddenly, allowing it to run out or *render* around a capstan, or the bitts, or cleat, etc.

The well-trained skipper and crew will not use oral instructions very often but will learn and practice the hand signals given later in this book.

Up killick means to desert.

Sandpaper the anchor was an order given to confuse or make fun of the neophyte, akin to asking for a left-handed monkey wrench, or a can of prop wash!

Swallow the anchor means to give up seafaring and move ashore.

To have an *anchor to windward* is the same as a nest egg, something to fall back on.

To *anchor one's stern* is to be seated.

The *hook* or *mud-hook* means any type of anchor.

To *put down the anchor* is to marry and settle down.

A *Dutchman's anchor* is something important that has been forgotten and left behind.

While the natural use of the correct word in any writing or speech is much to be desired, don't over do it! Too much *salt on the lips* is apt to make one stand out as some sort of nautical freak.

CHAPTER 2

Proper Ground Tackle

Many cruising skippers, it seems, have dangerous delusions concerning the selection and proper use of ground tackle. The subject, so essential to our sailing forefathers, is in danger of becoming a lost art. Even those who live aboard and cruise extensively sometimes become complacent and careless.

Perhaps part of the reason is the fault of insurance companies. Usually they will insure your boat without any inspection of its gear. In my own yacht insurance dealings, the subject of ground tackle never has come up. Those who cruise where insurance is impossible or too expensive to obtain, take out insurance in the form of ground tackle and knowledge.

Someday insurance companies may learn that it is not at sea where most accidents happen, but where water meets shore. Many of these accidents can be avoided by proper use of proper ground tackle.

Perhaps also, an element of disbelief is involved. Those sailors who don't cruise in the crystal-clear waters of places such as the Bahamas and the South Seas, never see their anchor doing its work. They merely drop it into the murky depths, where it is out of sight and thus out of mind.

Anchoring, broadly speaking, is the art and science of securely attaching your boat to the bottom.

In total calm and with no current, you will stay put without any anchor.

In a light breeze almost any weight on the bottom will hold you in place.

As the wind picks up, the need for better ground tackle increases.

In storm conditions, only the best will provide you with adequate security.

If you plan to anchor out only three or four times a year, you probably can choose your weather and get by with modest gear and limited knowledge of different anchoring techniques. However, most boat owners, especially those who go in for extended cruising, use their anchors quite frequently. And even if a sailor is careful in choosing his weather, that's no guarantee the weather will cooperate all the time. Encountering some heavy conditions is unavoidable and thus we need the best of gear and the knowledge of how to use it.

Having established that proper ground tackle not only is desirable but absolutely essential, let's consider the different gear that is involved.

Keep in mind that most of the discussion here will be about ground tackle for storm conditions. If it works well under storm conditions, it certainly will serve for anything less. It's up to you to decide how well you should prepare for storms.

THINK SYSTEM!

One important aspect of anchoring that must never be forgotten is that the anchor itself is only one element of the entire anchoring system. All parts of the system must be adequately strong and compatible. One weak link makes the entire system deficient. One incompatible component may render the system difficult or even impossible to use, particularly when it's needed most.

A typical system consists of anchor, shackle or swivel (or both), rode (be it chain, rope, cable or combination, including any knots or splices), chocks or hawse holes, windlass, cleats or Samson posts and stowage (for both anchor and rode). Other gear also is used in the anchoring process, for example the dinghy, but it is not, of itself, part of the ground tackle.

Any of these can be a weak link. Typically it may be a shackle or knot. More on this later.

A well-equipped yacht will have several anchoring systems but, of course, not spare windlasses, chocks, cleats, etc. Usually each system is dedicated to a specific use, such as anchoring on different bottoms. You can't always choose the bottom where you must anchor, so you should be able to select an appropriate anchor from among those carried.

ANCHORS

There exist three distinct, generic categories of anchors. One derives its holding power principally due to its weight. Examples are the mushroom and the navy anchors. They are rarely used for yachts, except as permanent moorings, as their holding power is very low in proportion to their weight.

The second group is used because of its ability to hook onto something on the bottom, be it coral, shells, rocks or shale. Examples are the grapnel, the fisherman, the SAV.

The third group depends on its ability to dig into the bottom and bury itself. Its effectiveness is a function of how readily it does this. Its holding power when properly buried is in proportion to its effective fluke area and the kind of

25

material in which it is buried. This group includes the Danforth Lightweight, the CQR plow, the Bruce and the Northill.

The Danforth Lightweight is a particular type of anchor that has been copied over and over again. It is offered by Danforth in several versions, which we shall mention further. I recommend the original Danforth over any of the copies and the high tensile over any other Danforth version in current production.

Some anchors are good at both hooking and burying, in varying degrees. Among these are the fisherman, the Northill, the Bruce and some others.

The criteria of a satisfactory anchor are: strength, ability to avoid fouling, effective fluke area, burying ability, stowing convenience and ease of handling.

STRUCTURAL STRENGTH

This criteria is as important as burying or hooking capability. What good is an anchor that has hooked on or buried itself adequately, then bends and pulls out, or breaks under strain.

Strength is achieved by design and selection of materials and manufacturing method.

Forged steel is stronger than cast.

Cast steel is generally stronger than welded steel.

Arc-welded steel is stronger than spot welded.

Size for size, steel is stronger than aluminum. For example, a forged plow such as the original CQR generally is much stronger than a cast or welded copy. An aluminum anchor may have a high ratio of holding power to weight, but is it strong enough for the most severe conditions?

Although weight itself has very little to do with successful anchoring, it is a very important feature of both burying and hooking types. The burying types must cut through the surface "crust," or through weeds, in order to bury into the bottom. Some try to manage with less weight by providing sharpened edges to the flukes. This will help, but there is no substitute for weight.

In an anchor intended primarily for hooking, strength can only be achieved through weight.

In neither type does the weight hold you in place. However, manufacturers rarely rate or advertise their anchors in terms of pounds of holding power or effective fluke area. They catalog them by weight in pounds or kilograms. Most manufacturers do advertise and recommend the size anchor to buy for certain sizes of yachts. They cannot be expected to guess what bottom condition and extreme of weather you will be encountering, so any recommendation is at best only an approximation. And all are biased towards their own product, which is only natural. In any event, would you trust your yacht and your life to an advertising copy writer?

Any table giving recommended anchor sizes based on yacht weight or yacht length essentially is meaningless.

It can be used only as a starting point for consideration of the size and type of ground tackle you should put on your yacht.

FOULING TENDENCY

Any anchor is apt to become fouled in debris on the bottom but some tend to foul their own rodes as the yacht swings in the shifting wind or tide. This kind of fouling results in the strain being placed on the anchor from the wrong direction and may cause it to break out.

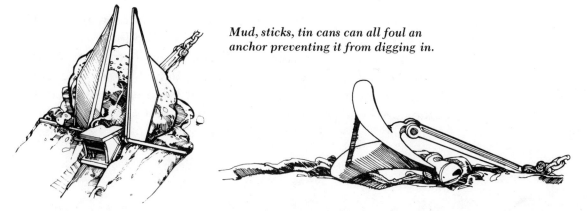

Mud, sticks, tin cans can all foul an anchor preventing it from digging in.

Probably the worst anchor for self-fouling is the fisherman type, which leaves one fluke sticking up out of the bottom at all times. As the boat swings, the rode winds itself around the exposed fluke. To some extent grapnels and the Northill exhibit much the same problem. Even the Danforth and other lightweight copies have been known to foul their rodes around the crown.

The CQR and Bruce rarely, if ever, foul like this.

EFFECTIVE FLUKE AREA

This criterion has a great bearing on the holding power of a burying anchor. It is not a measurable number but is a figure representing the fluke area in proportion to the anchor's weight. It is a feature you can estimate reasonably when comparing different anchors. Obviously a Bruce or a Danforth has greater fluke area than a fisherman of the same weight, and the latter more than a grapnel.

BURYING ABILITY

Anchors such as the lightweight, the CQR and the Bruce are popular because of the ease with which they enter the bottom. The lightweight and the CQR may have difficulty if there is extensive weed cover. They tend to skate across the weeds. The fisherman is an excellent anchor for use where heavy kelp is found. More weight will always help, as will sharper cutting edges of the flukes.

The deeper the anchor buries, the harder it is to break out, adding to your security. Some anchors are fitted with an eye in the crown to which a line may be attached for retrieval.

Should the boat swing over a wide arc while exerting strain on the rode, there is danger of accidental break out. The lightweight types seem to break out more easily (and occasionally bend or break the shank) than the CQR or Bruce but in good bottom conditions they all usually reset themselves.

HOW A CQR SETS

· DRAGS SLOWLY ON SIDE

SHAPE OF PLOUGH
TURNS SO POINT
CAN DIG IN

CONTINUED MOVE—
MENT SUB—
MERGES PLOUGH ENTIRELY

You should always be prepared to take action when your boat swings extensively or prevent such swinging from taking place.

CONVENIENCE OF STOWING

It is essential that the anchor be capable of being stowed where it is convenient and ready for instant use. It must not create hazards for those moving about the foredeck, nor provide sharp corners to tear sails or tangle lines.

The CQR and the Bruce are very easy to stow on a properly designed bow roller but are very difficult to stow in any other place.

29

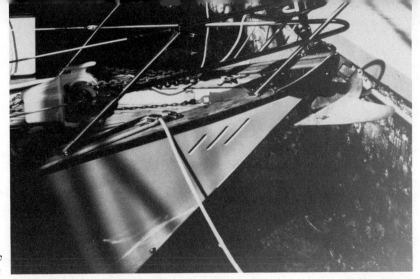

It is more common to stow a CQR in a bow roller but it can also be stowed under the bowsprit.

A Bruce stows conveniently in a bow roller.

a

b

c

d

Lightweight anchors are usually stowed (a) **attached to the pulpit, or** (b) **on the cabin top, or** (c) **tied to the aft railing, convenient for emergency use.** (d) **The best arrangement is through a hawse hole and pipe.**

31

The lightweight types are, of necessity, stowed flat on deck, lashed to the shrouds, or hung from the pulpit. I personally don't like any of these locations and the best I have found for this type is pulled into a hawse pipe—quite practical on metal hulls, very difficult to accomplish on fiberglass or wooden hulls.

Most fishermen, the SAV and the Northill either come apart or fold up for stowing. Be sure it can be made ready on very short notice in an emergency.

The fisherman can be stowed, (a) lashed on deck, (b) on the bulwark and attached to the cat-head as in this large schooner, or (c) folded and securely lashed to the rail, or (d) attached to the bowsprit.

a

b

c

d

The SAV folds for stowage but fits this bow roller ready for use. (I consider the aluminum bowsprit and roller very unsatisfactory. In rough anchoring circumstances it could be broken off. There is far too much overhang.)

Then there are the deck stowage lockers, which are tidy, if nothing else. They have several disadvantages, which should be taken into consideration.

The locker design limits the type and size of anchor you can stow.

Anchor lockers in the foredeck offer neat stowage arrangements, but with some serious restrictions.

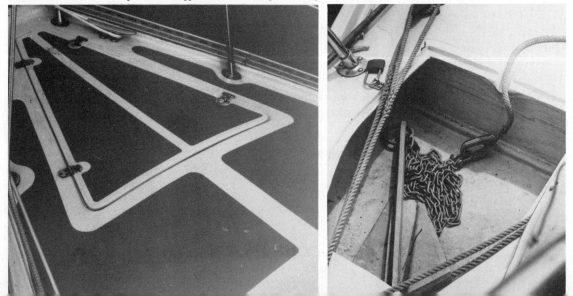

A large opening in the foredeck may be a serious hazard to those who must work up there, either lowering or weighing the anchor, especially when the anchor is needed most—in storm conditions.

Danger exists that some of the water taken into such lockers during a blow will find its way below. Mike Saunders, writing in *Practical Boat Owner* (February, 1984), describes delivering a modern 37-footer across the Bay of Biscay in a severe storm. The anchor wells allowed more than 100 gallons of water to enter the boat, trimming the bow down severely and adding greatly to the problems encountered on the trip.

EASE OF HANDLING

Considering various types, all of the same weight, an anchor with fewer moving parts, with the weight more or less concentrated, and with minimum projections, will be the easiest to handle. By these standards, then, the easiest is the Bruce, followed closely by the CQR and the lightweight. At the other end of the scale is the Northill and the fisherman.

Most anchors will rise and fall straight. The lightweights, however, have an annoying habit called "kiting," referring to

"Kiting" is a disadvantage of some anchor styles, particularly the lightweight pattern.

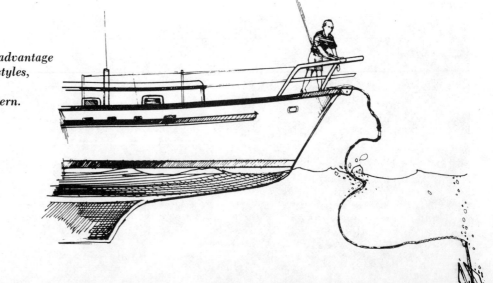

It is hard to find space to stow an unwieldy anchor below decks. This one fits in a shelf in the heads and is securely lashed in place.

the anchor's tendency to slide off to one side when being lowered or raised at a moderate rate of speed.

Any anchor that automatically comes up over the bow roller and self-stows is naturally easier to handle than one that doesn't. This advantage depends as much on the design of the bow roller as on the anchor. Again, the Northill and the fisherman trail the pack in this matter. Probably the easiest to handle is a lightweight or plow, especially if they stow in a well-designed hawse pipe.

When you are off soundings, where there is no possible need for your anchor to be "at the ready," you may wish to bring it below and lash it securely, well out of the way.

As you approach an anchorage, you may find it advantageous to lower the anchor just off the roller and suspend it, ready for immediate action.

You must also consider where you are going to stow your second, third or fourth anchors. The limit for stowing on the bow rollers really is two.

Wherever you store your anchors, on deck or below, stow them securely. Lash them down well. Should an anchor come loose in foul weather, it can cause very serious injury or damage.

35

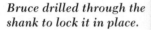
Bruce drilled through the shank to lock it in place.

Be sure the anchors stored below can be found and brought on deck quickly in the event they are needed unexpectedly.

I've noticed quite a number of plow-style anchors drilled through the shank to take a pin. This pin may indeed lock the anchor securely to the bow roller assembly but it may also dangerously weaken the anchor.

THE PROBLEM OF THEFT

This is probably a good place to touch briefly on an unpleasant subject, that of ground tackle theft. It happens more fre-

A CQR locked to the bow roller.

quently than one would like to think. If you must leave your boat unoccupied in a berth or at dockside, be sure to take appropriate precautions. Padlock each anchor securely. Do not leave bundles of rope on deck.

While at anchor, I don't know what to suggest. Anchors still on deck are vulnerable and I know of one sailor who had his anchor stolen off the end of the rode while it was on the bottom.

Unfortunately, it appears the worst offenders are other boating people. It's a crime akin to stealing the cowboy's horse, perhaps worthy of lynching. The life—as well as the property—of the victim is jeopardized.

Another problem is vandalism. Rodes have been cut at times. A chain is much less susceptible to this problem than rope. The only solution is a full-time anchor watch. I must lead a sheltered life (knock on fiberglass!) but so far, I've been the victim of neither theft nor vandalism.

COMPARING ANCHOR PERFORMANCE

Let's briefly compare some of the more popular styles of anchors in use today.

THE LIGHTWEIGHT

The lightweight pattern is probably the most common type in the Americas. It is manufactured in the U.S by Danforth, Viking and others and in the U.K. by Meon and others.

An excellent anchor for hard sand (some say the best), it has large fluke area for given weight and buries readily, providing the pull is from horizontal to not more than 8° from the bottom. This necessitates a rather high scope ratio. A length of chain attached to the anchor is almost a necessity. The holding power in soft mud is only about 20% of that in hard sand, but this holds true for most anchors.

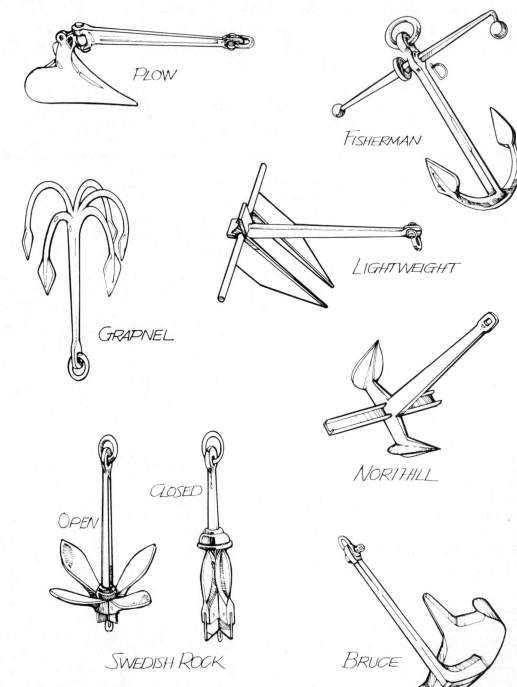

PLOW

FISHERMAN

GRAPNEL

LIGHTWEIGHT

NORTHILL

OPEN

CLOSED

NORTHILL

38

SWEDISH ROCK

BRUCE

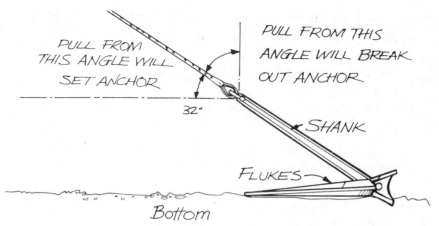

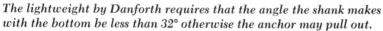

The lightweight by Danforth requires that the angle the shank makes with the bottom be less than 32° otherwise the anchor may pull out.

In heavy weed, the lightweight tends to skate across the bottom. In rocks, shell or coral, it is vulnerable as it does not have the necessary strength unless one selects the "high tensile" version, or uses a particularly heavy one.

The lightweight tends to break out easily if the strain comes from a much different direction to that in which it was set. Also it is subject to fouling more easily than some others. The rode may get wrapped around the crown. A stick, stone, tin can, or even large chunks of clay may jam between flukes

A spot-welded lightweight bent and broken apart by excessive strain when caught by a squall while anchored in coral.

39

and stock and prevent penetration. Likewise, anything that catches on the tip of either fluke prevents the anchor from embedding itself in the bottom.

It is difficult to find a good arrangement for stowing a lightweight on a bow roller and I personally do not like to see them hanging from the pulpit. If there is room on deck, they readily can be stowed flat. A large one may conveniently be secured to the mainmast rigging. Perhaps the best arrangement is pulled up into a hawse pipe.

The lightweight deserves its popularity. Taking everything into account, it is an excellent anchor. The high tensile Danforth version is best.

THE FISHERMAN

This is a refined version of a very early type of anchor. Credit goes to Herreshoff for the most recent refinement. Many call it a kedge, though I believe this is erroneous. It is one of the most successful types of anchors though somewhat hard to find today. In my own experience, it has never failed to hook on and hold tight.

They are particularly good as a hook in coral, shale, rocks, etc., providing the flukes are large enough. Larger flukes, however, means more weight. They also are excellent for anchoring in hard mud and clay. They have better penetration in heavy weed cover than most others.

Most are capable of being dismantled or folded for stow-

The fisherman is a very satisfactory and popular hooking anchor. Some models disassemble for stowage. Some fold as does this Stowaway bronze fisherman. Photo courtesy Sea Anchors Ltd.

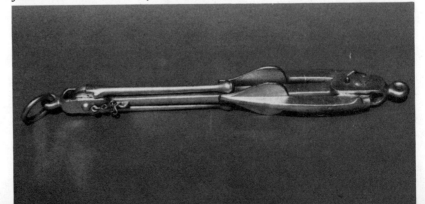

40

age. My own, of unknown make, can be assembled in well under a minute. When not on soundings, it stores in the bilge.

It will set with a relatively short scope, but it is difficult to handle and bring up over the side without marring the hull.

Important features to look for are wide flukes, sharp cutting edges, well faired back edge of flukes (to reduce the tendency to foul the rode), strength and weight.

THE GRAPNEL

Grapnels, such as the cast steel SAV and the common 5-prong version made of steel rod do have a definite place in your ground tackle. They are fine in rock and coral, shells and the like. They cut easily through kelp and other weed, but the flukes are too narrow to give much holding power when buried. The flukes left standing upright are very vulnerable to fouling the rode.

A grapnel works better than any other type for dragging for some object lost overboard.

The SAV folds and is easy to stow. Stowing all grapnels on a yacht is next to impossible.

The SAV makes a good shore anchor for it is usually easy to drive one fluke into the ground.

A simple shore hook grapnel can be made of ⅜" or ½" steel rod that can be pushed or driven into the ground. I have not seen such a device on the market.

A simple hook for anchoring to shore can be made up as illustrated. Alternatively a "corkscrew" of the type sold in pet stores to "anchor" your dog may work well.

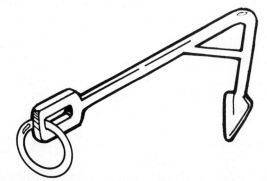

41

The plow, of which the most common type is the CQR, is a hot-forged anchor of extreme strength. The same company, Simpson Lawrence, makes a cast anchor in the lighter weights and there are many copies made of fabricated and welded steel. I don't believe any of them approach the strength of the forged version CQR. Get it whenever possible in preference to any copy.

The plow is excellent in all types of sand, mud, and clay, but tends to experience difficulty in penetrating heavy weed cover such as kelp. I have used it successfully in rock or coral, though I prefer my fisherman for this type of bottom.

It has a high effective fluke area and excellent holding power with very little tendency towards being accidentally pulled out as the direction of strain changes. If it should, it will generally reset itself in the direction of the new strain.

It will not foul its own rode or rarely foul with stones, clay or debris, but may pick up a can or cable as will most types of anchors.

It is very easy to stow on a bow roller but rather inconvenient to stow on deck or down below. In a survey of experienced cruising people, the CQR is rated as the top or first choice by most.

Some consider the lightweight anchor superior in sand. Perhaps it is. My experience with the CQR has been excellent. Once we were anchored at the mouth of the Cohansey River on my 35 lb. CQR, waiting out foul weather, with friends aboard *Mischief* anchored not far away with a 35 lb. lightweight. We were wakened in the night by a crash as the two boats hit. *Mischief* had dragged down on us in the rising wind. After repeated attempts to get his anchor set securely, he gave up and rafted alongside us. Although the winds were moderately strong, even though we were in protected waters, our CQR held both boats firmly until the next morning. The bottom was more mud than sand in this instance.

THE NORTHILL

This is a very acceptable anchor providing it is well made. Some are fabricated from steel plate, or stainless steel, spot welded and pinned (or bolted) together. I would have no hesitation in recommending a well made Northill for any soft bottom and believe it is an acceptable hook for rock or coral, as well. However, I do not like spot-welded construction in an anchor.

The fluke area is relatively high in proportion to the weight. One fluke sticks up and creates a potential fouling hazard for the rode as the yacht swings.

Folding versions are easy to stow but it is a difficult anchor to haul aboard without scratching the topsides.

THE BRUCE

This anchor is a relative newcomer on the scene but has already gained very high popularity.

It has excellent holding power in sand and mud and requires a relatively short scope. It will not foul its rode and needs low force to break out. It is good at hooking as well as burying and is easy to handle and stow on a bow roller, though difficult to stow on deck or down below.

It has no moving parts and is exceptionally strong and easy to handle.

Robert Smith, in his book, *Anchor Selection And Use*, reported the Bruce would not set in one trial as a "large, hard-packed accumulation of sand was caught between its three-lobed fluke and the crook of the shank. This condition recurred on successive trials."

The Bruce deserves every consideration as an addition to your ground tackle.

The above briefly describes most of the popular anchors used by experienced skippers. Good ones are expensive and there are much cheaper anchors on the market, but steer

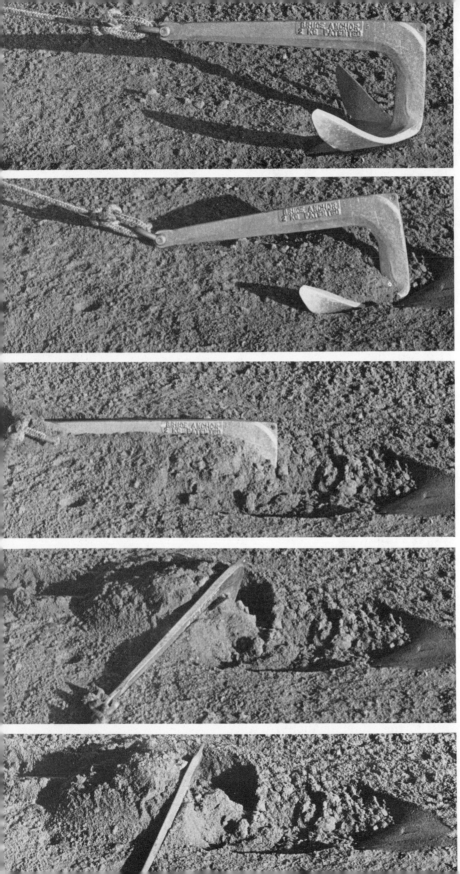

The Bruce grips quickly. The side flukes are designed so that the anchor becomes embedded in three lengths of the shank. As the anchor is in one piece, if the wind veers 90° when it is embedded. it will pivot on the vertical shank without losing its grip. Photos courtesy South Western Marine Factors Ltd.

COMPARISON OF SOME COMMON ANCHORS

Anchor	Type	Burying Effectiveness	Hooking Effectiveness	Efficiency in Weeds	Tendency to Foul	Effective Fluke Area	Danger of Accidental Breakout	Ease of Handling[1]	Ease of Stowing[1]
Danforth Lightweight	burying	high	low	low	moderate	high	moderate	moderate	moderate
Bruce	burying	high	low	moderate	nil	high	low	high	high
CQR Plow	burying	high	low	moderate	nil	high	low	high	high
Fisherman	hooking	moderate	high	high	high	low	moderate	low	high (when folded or disassembled)
Northill	burying	high	moderate	high	high	moderate	moderate	low	high (when folded)
SAV	hooking	low	high	moderate	high	low	high	moderate	high (when folded)
Grapnel	hooking	nil	high	low	high	low	high	low	nil
Mushroom	burying	high	nil	nil	nil	n/a	high	low	nil

[1]Assumes a vessel equipped with proper bow roller or similar fittings.

45

clear of the latter. Follow William G. Van Dorn's excellent advice in his book, *Oceanography And Seamanship* (Dodd, Mead & Co., 1974): "Good anchors cost more, but not as much as good boats."

The serious cruising skipper will equip his yacht with three, four or five complete anchor systems. I carry a CQR, three sizes of Danforth lightweights and a fisherman—all good anchors. If I was forced to choose only one, I would have difficulty.

OTHER NOTEWORTHY ANCHORS

Several anchors, less well known to me, are on the market and must be considered along with the more popular brands and types.

THE SUPERB

Made by Sea Grip AB in Sweden, this anchor appears to be a hooking/burying type in the fashion of a fisherman, but folds into quite a small space for storage. It should work well in weeds, rocks and coral. It has a larger fluke area than the fisherman so may be satisfactory in mud and clay as well. It

The "Superb" Sea Grip Anchor from Sweden.

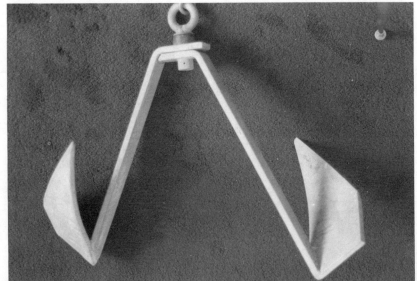

The "Crab Claw" plastic encased anchor.

is offered in weights of 3 kg (6.6 lbs.), 6 kg (13.23 lbs.), 10 kg (20.5 lbs.) and 15 kg (33 lbs.).

It seems to me it would be subject to rode fouling, but if you require a fisherman type, you may want to consider it.

THE CRAB CLAW

This is a newly introduced anchor made of plastic with encased ballast. I haven't tested, nor seen any test results for the Crab Claw. Without some very substantial information on its holding qualities, I would hesitate to recommend it for any boat larger than a small rowboat.

THE PRIORITY

Another anchor that seems to warrant much greater consideration has been developed and patented by David Prior of Lunenburg, Nova Scotia, and named the Priority anchor. Prior has attempted to design a compromise between a fisherman hooking anchor and a burying anchor such as the lightweight. It is, of course, a compromise but has these features in its favor: strength, minimal rode fouling danger, breaks

47

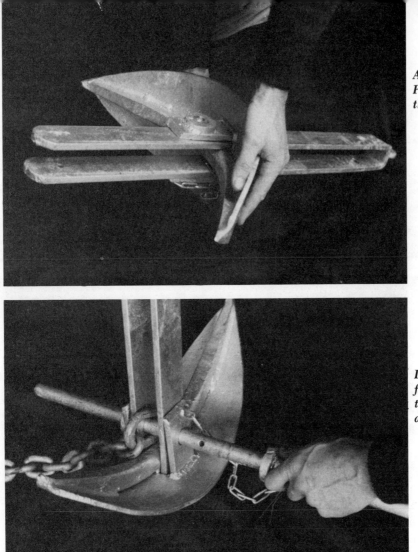

*Assembling a 40 lb.
Priority. Join the fluke to
the shank.*

*Insert stock to secure
fluke to shank and
to secure the end of the
anchor chain.*

*Run chain up the shank
and secure with a shear
pin.*

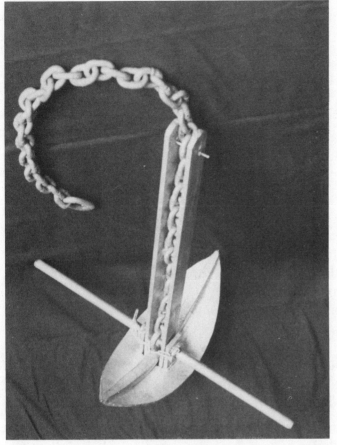

Fully assembled.

down for storage, yet assembles easily and is relatively inexpensive.

It can be disassembled and stored below or it can be stowed in a bow roller. It can be put into a dinghy in pieces and assembled at the anchoring point, thus permitting a heavier anchor to be used for a kedge.

It has a reliable self-tripping feature, essentially a built-in system for becueing. Calibrated sheer pins are offered with appropriate breaking strength. It reportedly hooks into cobblestone and similar bottoms more readily than does a lightweight. I do not know how it would perform in kelp or other heavy weed, but I expect it would have excellent weed-cutting ability, much like a fisherman.

49

This anchor is a French version of the lightweight, but with extra large fluke area. Some interesting tests results are reported for the FOB HP in the upcoming section "Which Anchor is Best?"

GENERAL NOTES

Fit the largest size of anchor you can stow and handle. Going up one size does not add much weight to the total system, but that extra weight, extra fluke area and extra strength may make all the difference in the world when you're hard-pressed one day.

Rarely can you be sure of anchoring in ideal bottom conditions.

However, you must also take into account the crew strength available to handle your ground tackle. With a good windlass relatively little muscle power is needed. But what if the windlass fails when it is needed most? Can you cope without it? Learn now to handle the gear without power assist, just in case.

The French lightweight version, the FOB HP.

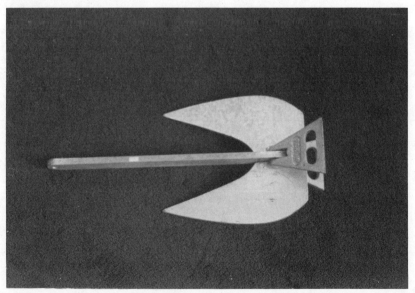

50

Calculating The Load On Ground Tackle

The holding power of the ground tackle must exceed the force of wind and current, including gusts of wind and actions of waves, or the anchor will drag. It must be obvious that the forces against the boat are essentially equal to the pull on the anchor and to the strain on the rode, shackles, cleats, etc.

It is possible to estimate with reasonable accuracy the total load to which a boat may be subjected. Divide the load into three parts, as follows:

1. Wind drag, the load resulting from the combination of wind pressure and suction on the superstructure, rigging and that part of the hull above water.
2. Current drag, caused by current on the hull and fittings below water.
3. Wave action.

Sum of forces on anchor and rode.

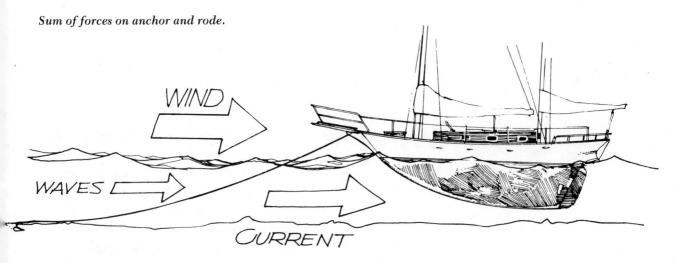

Wind force, or drag as it is referred to in aerodynamics, is determined by wind velocity, air density and shape of the object in the windstream. Although the first correlation of these factors was published by Sir Isaac Newton as early as 1686, it is only because of aviation research that it is possible now to accurately predict air drag for various objects. The formula for drag, "D," in pounds per square foot, is:

$$D = C_d \frac{\rho V^2 S}{2}$$

where ρ is the density of air,

    V is the wind velocity in knots,
    S is the cross-sectional area taken at right angles to the direction of the wind, in square feet.
    C_d is the coefficient of drag that varies with shape or profile.

Typical values for C_d are:

- Streamlined passenger liner, wind dead ahead, 0.70
- Pleasure boat, wind dead ahead, 0.70 to 1.0
- Airplane, 0.09

For the average-size pleasure boat, a figure of 0.80 is satisfactory. A boat with a really sleek superstructure will run as low as 0.70 while a blocky pilothouse might raise the figure to 1.00. Since most cruising yachts will carry a variety of deck cargo such as a dinghy, and in order to err on the side of safety, if at all, I suggest a figure of 1.0 is appropriate.

For ρ we will substitute the U.S. standard atmospheric air density of 0.0023779.

We came up with these figures for wind speed in knots and drag in pounds per square foot from the formula given above:

Wind speed	Drag
10	0.33
20	1.30
30	3.00
40	5.40
50	8.40
60	12.00
70	15.20
80	20.10

Note that as wind speed doubles, drag quadruples.

We must now calculate the projected cross-sectional area for the yacht looking at it from 30 degrees off the bow (to allow for the way in which the boat will yaw under typical storm conditions) and multiply the area arrived at by the drag figures from the above table.

You will want to go through these calculations for your own boat as I have done below for mine, which is a 32-foot, 6-ton ketch.

Hull 32′ x 4″ (average freeboard) x 0.5 (sine of 30)	64
Cabin 12 x 1.5 x 0.5	9
Dodger 4 x 1.5 x 0.5	3
Weather cloths 2 x 6 x 0.5	6
Mainmast 35 x 0.6	21
Main boom (sails furled) 8 x 0.75 x 0.5	4.5
Mizzenmast 22 x 0.5	11
Mizzen boom (sails furled) 8 x 0.75 x 0.5	3
Dinghy on cabin top 7.5 x 1.5 x 0.5	6
Lifelines, stanchions, pulpits (fore and aft), shrouds, standing and running rigging (estimate)	20
	188

For a wind speed of 40 knots, the wind drag will be 5.4 x 188 = 1015 pounds and for 80 knots, it will be 20.10 x 188 = 3779 pounds.

In comparison, current drag is of much less importance. For the same yacht, it is safe to add another 10%. For a larger yacht, you may want to increase this allowance.

Wave action is of even less importance providing you have incorporated some means of reducing snubbing. The sudden strain caused by snubbing is what usually breaks out an anchor or damages gear.

Our discussion centers around what may be called "normal anchoring" in a bay or lagoon with relatively short fetch. Under these conditions, wave action should not be serious.

Should you have to anchor in an open roadstead, however, or wherever the waves get up to any appreciable size, then wave action may be serious. Boats that rock severely at anchor, or "hobbyhorse," should incorporate an all-chain rode and/or an efficient riding weight into the anchoring system.

The information given here on anchor and rode strains is adequate for anyone except, perhaps, the technologists among us. For greater detail and more complex formulae, refer to *Oceanography And Seamanship* by William G. Van Dorn (Dodd, Mead & Co. 1974).

WHICH ANCHOR IS BEST?

To my knowledge, and I've searched the literature extensively, there have been no independent, scientific tests made on anchors of the size yachtsmen are apt to use. Such tests would have to compare different anchors in different bottoms. Lacking such tests, no really definite comparisons can be made.

An article was published in *L'auto-Journal* in Paris, France many years ago and reprinted in *Yachting Monthly* in the early 1970s after being translated into English and converted from metric numbering to Imperial. The relevant tables, supplied by Simpson Lawrence Ltd., makers of the CQR, are reprinted here.

We do not know how the tests were run and to what extent they can be considered authoritative. They are included for

Name of anchor	Weight (to nearest pound)	Distance anchor dragged before holding	Resistance in sand and mud (lb)	Resistance in sand and shingle (lb)	Clay (lb)	Total resistance (lb)	Efficiency factor
Genuine CQR anchor	16	3′ 5″	937	772	1146	2855	178·4
French CQR type anchor	23	5′ 3″	1157	66	1168	2391	103·9
Danforth anchor	16	1′ 9″	816	573	982	2370	148·1
			551	463			
Fisherman type anchor	26	3′ 3″	(1 time out of 5)	(1 time out of 2)	662	1676	64·4
Fisherman type anchor	19	3′ 5″	287	132	386	805	42·3
				121			
Tri-grip anchor	22	11″	375	(1 time out of 6)	309	805	36·5
German CQR type anchor	22	Did not hold	55	22	22	99	4·5

For further comparison of efficiency tests of types of Continental and other anchors carried out by the staff of *L'Auto Journal*, the complete table of results, converted from metric to English figures, is reproduced here by courtesy of Simpson-Lawrence Ltd.

your own interpretation. Simpson Lawrence Ltd. advised me it has not run any similar tests.

I have asked several manufacturers about their testing procedures. Most manufacturers are reluctant to disclose their testing methods, so the consumer must draw his own conclusion. The following tables are supplied by various manufacturers. If used judiciously, they might provide information otherwise unavailable to a yachtsman.

In 1979 tests were run in France by L'A.P.A.V.E., which is an organization somewhat similar to Underwriter's Laboratories in the US and to the Canadian Standards Association.

The results of the tests were published in the French magazine *Bateaux*. They appear to have been run as professionally as any I have seen and it is difficult to fault them, as far as they go.

The report is too long to include here. I have translated it to the best of my ability and have edited another's translation.

Seven anchors were run through the first series of tests, held in the bay of Saint Brieuc, France.

The anchors were attached to the end of a rode 118 feet long made of ⁵⁄₁₆″ chain. The strain was applied by a 33-foot

The aluminum lightweight Viking anchor.

ANCHOR PERFORMANCE COMPARISON
(Furnished by Viking)

Mfg'r. —	Model	Average Boat Length (ft.)	Approx. Weight (lbs.)	Horizontal[1] Holding Power (lbs.)	Test Strength[2] in sand (lbs.)	Rated Capacity (lbs.)
Benson	4	0–12	3.6			
Danforth	2½ S	0–9	2.5	800	510	
Keepers	4	0–12	4.0			
Viking	10	0–10	1.0	1000	790	400
Benson	6	15	5.0			
Danforth	4 S	10–16	4.0	1600	820	
Danforth	4 SR	10–16	4.0			
Keepers	6	15	6.0			
Viking	15	11–15	2.0	1700	1130	700
Benson	9	23	8.0			
Danforth	8 S	17–24	8.0	3200	920	
Danforth	9 SR	17–24	9.0			
Danforth	5 H	17–24	5.0	2700		
Keepers	10	25	10.0			
Viking	20	16–20	4.0	3500	1740	1000
Benson	12	28	11.0			
Benson	18	32	14.5			
Danforth	13 S	25–32	13.0	4200	3650	
Danforth	16 SR	25–32	16.0			
Keepers	15	30	15.0			
Viking	30	21–30	7.5	5000	4520	2000
Benson	26	36	22			
Benson	36	40	28			
Danforth	12 H	25–38	12	6000		
Danforth	22 S	33–38	22	8000	(See Note 3)	
Keepers	24	40	24			
Viking	40	31–40	12.25	8000	6130	4000
Danforth	20 H	39–44	20	8750		
Danforth	40 S	39–44	40	10000	(See Note 4)	
Keepers	36	50	36			
Viking	50	41–50	20	10000	5200	5000
Danforth	35 H	45–54	35	11000		
Danforth	65S	45–54	65	15000	10500	
Viking	60	51–60	33.5	12000	12166	6000

SOURCE: Manufacturer's Literature (1973).
    1. Manufacturer's data for strength in hard sand.
    2. Strength determined in test tank using water-immersed sand. Tests certified by Notary Public and Tropical Marine Testers, Inc.
    3. Anchor's crown top weld broke during test.
    4. Anchor bent beyond use during test.

| VIKING ANCHOR | | | | | | ESTIMATED HORIZONTAL DESIGN LOAD ON ANCHORS FOR VARIOUS BOAT LENGTHS AND ANCHORING CONDITIONS* | | | | STRENGTH OF NYLON YACHT ROPE AND CHAIN RECOMMENDED | | | | |
| Size | Weight | Test Strength | **Rated Capacity | Overall Length | Overall Width | Perm. Mooring | Storm Anchor | Working Anchor | Lunch Hook | NYLON YACHT ROPE | | BBB GALV. COIL CHAIN | | |
										Size	Strength	Size	Strength	Length
NO. 10	1#	1,000#	400#	18"	14⅞"	480#	320#	160#	40#	¼"	425#	¼"	1,300#	3'
NO. 15	2#	1,700#	700#	20⅛"	15"	750#	500#	250#	60#	5/16"	700#	¼"	1,300#	4'
NO. 20	4#	3,500#	1,000#	24½"	18"	1,080#	720#	360#	90#	3/8"	1,000#	¼"	1,300#	5'
NO. 30	7½#	5,000#	2,000#	28¾"	22"	2,100#	1,400#	700#	175#	9/16"	2,000#	3/8"	2,800#	6'
NO. 40	12¼#	8,000#	4,000#	37"	27"	3,600#	2,400#	1,200#	300#	¾"	3,500#	7/16"	3,600#	7'
NO. 50	20#	10,000#	5,000#	43⅝"	31"	4,800#	3,200#	1,600#	400#	7/8"	4,800#	½"	4,700#	8'
NO. 60	33½#	12,000#	6,000#	52#⅞"	38"	6,000#	4,000#	2,000#	500#	1"	6,000#	5/8"	7,000#	9'

*The test strengths shown above were obtained by pulling the anchors thru water immersed sand in the test tank shown above, and recording the values shown on the calibrated dynamometer attached to the anchor traveler. Assuming average conditions of exposure current—and freedom of boat oscillation with the waves. Working strengths with a safety factor of 4 for the nylon rope and 2 for the chain.
**In sand with 7 to 1 scope.

TYPICAL DESIGN HORIZONTAL LOADS IN POUNDS

L.O.A. (1)	Beam (1)		Permanent Mooring	Storm Anchor	Working Anchor	Lunch Hook
	Sail	Power (2)				
10	4	5	480	320	160	40
15	5	6	750	500	250	60
20	7	8	1080	720	360	90
25	8	9	1470	980	490	125
30	9	11	2100	1400	700	175
35	10	13	2700	1800	900	225
40	11	14	3600	2400	1200	300
50	13	16	4800	3200	1600	400
60	15	18	6000	4000	2000	500

NOTES: (1) When using this table with the length overall or beams, use whichever gives the highest load, assuming freedom to oscillate is permitted and moderate shelter from seas proportionate to hull size.
(2) Houseboats should use the load one category higher than that determined by using the power boat column.

Recommendations courtesy American Boat and Yacht Council.

HORIZONTAL HOLDING POWER OF DANFORTH® ANCHORS IN POUNDS

	Soft Mud	Hard Sand
5-H	400	2,700
12-H	900	6,000
20-H	1,250	8,750
35-H	1,600	11,000
60-H	2,400	17,000
90-H	2,900	20,000
200-H	5,000	35,000
500-H	7,500	50,000
3000-H	21,000	140,000
2½-S	140	800
4-S	230	1,600
8-S	480	3,200
13-S	720	4,900
22-S	1,200	8,000
40-S	1,500	10,000
65-S	2,300	15,000
85-S	2,700	19,000
130-S	3,100	21,000
180-S	3,500	23,000

SUGGESTED WORKING ANCHOR SIZES

Boat Length	Danforth® Standard Anchor	Danforth® Hi-Tensile Anchor
0–9	2½-S	—
10–16	4-S / 4-SR	—
17–24	8-S / 9-SR	5-H
25–32	13-S / 16-SR	12-H
33–38	22-S	12-H
39–44	40-S	20-H
45–54	65-S	35-H
55–70	85-S	60-H
71–90	130-S	90-H

For storm anchor, use one anchor size larger.
For lunch hook, one size smaller.

SUGGESTED CQR® WORKING ANCHOR SIZES

Weight approx.—lbs	15	20	25	35	45	60	75	105
kilos	6·8	9	11·3	15·8	20·4	27	34	48

Suggested size of craft—
Sailing yachts or light displacement motor craft:

Water line length (feet)	15	20	22	28	35	40	45	—

Full power motor craft:

Displacement (tons)	—	2	5	10	15	25	30	—

The above figures are given as a general guide only. The service for which it is required and the type of vessel must be taken into consideration in selecting the most suitable size.

Suggested Bruce® Working Anchor Sizes

Anchor Weight				Maximum Boat Dimensions			Recommended Rode						Alloy Steel Shackle			
Storm		Working		Length O.A.	Beam Sail	Beam Power	Nylon Rope Dia.		Chain Dia.		Chafing Chain Length		Pin Dia.		Body Dia.	
kg	lb	kg	lb	ft	ft	ft	mm	ins	mm	ins	m	ft	mm	ins	mm	ins
1	2.2	—	—	9	4.3	4.6	6	0.24	5	0.20	1.5	4.9	6	0.24	5	0.20
2	4.4	1	2.2	15	6.6	7.2	9	0.31	5	0.20	2.0	6.6	8	0.31	6	0.24
5	11	2	4.4	23	8.9	9.5	10	0.39	6	0.24	2.6	8.5	10	0.39	8	0.31
7.5	16.5	5	11	30	10.5	11.2	12	0.47	7	0.28	3.0	9.8	10	0.39	8	0.31
10	22	5	11	35	11.5	12.8	14	0.55	8	0.31	3.2	10.5	13	0.51	10	0.39
15	33	7.5	16.5	40	12.5	13.8	16	0.63	9	0.35	3.7	12.1	13	0.51	10	0.39
20	44	10	22	47	13.8	15.4	18	0.71	10	0.39	4.0	13.1	16	0.63	13	0.51
30	66	15	33	63	16.7	18.4	22	0.87	12	0.47	4.5	14.8	16	0.63	13	0.51
50	110	20	44	92	20.0	24	26	1.02	16	0.63	5.0	16.4	19	0.75	16	0.63

The anchor sizes given above assume winds up to 60 mph, some protection from the sea, fair holding ground, and operation at scope adequate to develop full-holding power. Vessels built to classification society requirements have anchor weights stipulated by the societies. For optimum performance a close fitting shackle should be used, otherwise the shackle should be centralized by means of galvanized washers. The mooring line should have sufficient elasticity to minimize shock loading on the anchor and on the boat fittings due to wind and wave surges. Chain of sufficient length to provide an adequate catenary, or nylon rope of sufficient length to provide an equivalent effect under load is recommended. Where nylon rope is used, a short length of chain should be included at the anchor end to resist chafing on the sea bed as recommended in the table above.

fishing boat equipped with a 180-hp. engine. Strain measuring instruments on the boat and other gear had a safe limit of 2040 pounds, well above the strain we would normally expect to encounter in yachts.

The water was 10–16 feet deep and the bottom is described as even, sandy, grown with short weeds.

A second series of tests were run under similar conditions in 16 feet of water on a bottom consisting of sand, mud and hard shells.

The purpose of the tests was to determine at what strain the anchors "tripped," i.e. pulled out of the bottom, and at what strain they "dragged," i.e. pulled through the bottom.

The anchors tested include three we know well in North America, the fisherman, the CQR and the Bruce. The other four all appear to be versions of the lightweight, invented and popularized by Danforth. Each of these four has its own particular design features though none include the stock, which is very much a feature of the Danforth lightweight.

These four bear the names, Brittany, FOB, FOB HP and Salle. (The Salle and the FOB are very much the same, by different manufacturers). All anchors tested were 26 lb. except the Bruce, which weighed 22 lb.

Note that six anchors were burying types and only one was a hooking type.

One important feature of the tests was that they were witnessed and photographed by a scuba diver.

Anchors	First Series		Second Series	
	Stress to Trip Lbs.	Drag, Low & High Lbs.	Stress to Trip Lbs.	Drag, Low & High Lbs.
Britany	1719	1014/1510	827	760/1433
FOB	617	242/297	not tested	not tested
CQR	did not trip, dragged.	1719/2039	518	881
FOB HP	2039. Did not trip.	Never dragged	1708	no measure
Bruce	507	198/242	595	no measure
Salle	705	308/407	507	198/298
Fisherman	352	198/242	not tested	not tested

Some explanation of the results shown in the table is in order.

The CQR did not trip during the tests, but at very high strains it plowed through the bottom.

The FOB HP neither tripped nor dragged. It appears to have just dug deeper into the bottom.

The Bruce appears to have performed very poorly. From underwater observations, the anchor ring on the end of the shank buried but the flukes had a tendency to lift.

The strains recorded on the fisherman were very much as we would have expected in this type of bottom.

At the request of the French distributor of Bruce anchors, a further series of tests were run comparing a 33 lb. Bruce, a 22 lb. Bruce and a 26 lb. FOB HP.

Testing procedures were essentially the same except the rode was 98 feet of line and 26 feet of chain. The bottom is described as a mixture of sand and mud and depth was 26 to 33 feet. The report admits that a higher scope ratio would have been more representative of proper anchoring tactics.

Again, neither size Bruce could hold the same strain as the FOB HP. However, the Bruce outperformed the other in swivel tests wherein the boat turned without reducing strain. The Bruce was able to pivot on itself without coming loose. The FOB HP turned with one fluke out of the bottom, although it still held well. A stock such as used in the Danforth design probably would have prevented this.

A further test was run with a 22 lb. Danforth high strength lightweight. The results indicated the FOB HP and the Danforth lightweight had essentially the same holding power under the testing circumstances and held to 1763 pounds strain.

The report indicates the FOB HP was easier to break out of the bottom on weighing and that the Danforth was so thoroughly dug in that assistance of the diver was required to release it.

Further, the FOB HP suffered some distortion whereas the Danforth lightweight did not.

One must not regard these tests as totally conclusive nor damn the Bruce out of hand. They do, however, indicate the FOB HP is an anchor worth serious consideration for use in burying conditions.

One can only conjecture at the test results. It is quite possible the Danforth lightweight and the FOB HP buried through the surface strata into deeper, harder, more consistent bottom material. This is precisely what they should do under such strains.

The CQR and the Bruce plowed through the surface material. In fact the photographs show the CQR ploughing a straight furrow and piling up bottom material on both sides. The photo of the Bruce, however, shows it pushing a great pile of bottom material ahead of it.

One cannot help but feel that test results furnished by manufacturers are apt to be somewhat biased. Results from one manufacturer cannot be compared directly with those of another as the quality of bottom and manner of testing may be quite different.

It would be interesting to see all anchors tested by an independent qualified organization, under scientific conditions and in various bottom conditions.

Lacking this, we must turn to another group of experts, who are certainly independent, if not completely unbiased, and who have had years of experience in actual use in all kinds of bottoms.

SOME EXPERT OPINIONS

Here is what some very experienced cruising people have included in their complement of ground tackle.

Eric Hiscock, who spent most of his life cruising, and who has gone around the world five or six times, had the following equipment on *Wanderer III* (30' LOA, 8½' beam, 8 tons displacement): Two 35 lb. CQR plow anchors, 45 fathoms of ⁵⁄₁₆" tested short link chain, 30 fathoms on one, 15 on the other, plus ½″ nylon, no windlass but chain pawl on the bow roller. His next boat, *Wanderer IV* was larger and heavier (49½′ LOA, 12½′ beam, 20 tons displacement). On her he carried one 75 lb. CQR plow with 45 fathoms of ½″ tested chain, a 45 lb. CQR with ⅜″ nylon, a 100 lb. fisherman. She was fitted with an electric windlass and a 7″ diameter bow roller.

Gorder and Nina Stuermer who sailed *Starbound* around the world (50′ on deck, 17′ beam, 35 tons) carried: 130 lb. fisherman on 450′ of ½″ chain, 70 lb. Danforth high tensile, with 20′ of ½″ chain and 300′ of ½″ eight-strand plaited nylon and a 35 lb. Danforth high tensile for the stern. He added a 105 lb. CQR and relegated the 70 lb. Danforth to the stern.

Bob Griffith on *Awahnee* (53′ LOA, 25 tons) had perhaps the largest inventory for a boat of that size:

Anchors	Weight (pounds)
CQR (plow)	25
2 welded stainless steel folding Northills	45
Herreshoff improved fisherman	40
Standard fisherman	40
Standard cast Northill	25
Collapsible grapnel	25
Stockless dinghy	10
Northill dinghy	6
Steel grapnel	6

Galvanized Chain	Length (fathoms)	Diameter (inches)
Main anchor	60	7/16
Long lead	10	7/16
Heavy lead	5	5/8
2 lengths	4 each	7/16
4 lengths	1 to 3 each	5/16
Dinghy chain	3½	3/16

Ropes And Lines	Length (fathoms)	Diameter (inches)
Main anchor (polypropylene)	60	1
Second (polypropylene)	50	3/4
Third (manila)	35	1
Reserve (polypropylene)	92	5/8

65

Hal Roth, renowned for his circumnavigation of the Pacific and for exploring the Chilean islands in *Whisper* (35′ LOA, 9½′ beam, 6 tons) carried: one 45 lb. CQR with 45 fathoms of ⅜″ chain, one 45 lb. CQR with one fathom chain and 45 fathoms of ¾″ nylon, one 42 lb. fisherman with one fathom chain and 33 fathoms of ⅝″ nylon. *Whisper* is also fitted with a hand-operated windlass. The total weight of ground tackle is 680 pounds.

The Pardeys, in 24′ *Seraffyn,* in which they sailed and lived for eight years in North American, European and Pacific waters, carry: One 22 lb. Danforth with 300′ of ⁵⁄₁₆″ chain and one 33 lb. fisherman with ⅝″ nylon. Later they added one 25 lb. CQR because they found the Danforth frequently fouled with pieces of coral and other debris, or fouled its own chain—all this on a 5½-ton yacht.

Ross Norgrove, in his 60-ton, 70′ schooner *White Squall II,* carried: A 150 lb. CQR with 60 fathoms of ⅝″ chain, a 200 lb. Northill with 45 fathoms of ⅝″ chain, an 85 lb. Danforth and a 40 lb. Northill. For the latter two, he attached 50-fathom lengths of 1″ nylon rode. The yacht is fitted with a hydraulic windlass for these heavy anchors.

Tom Colvin, in 42′ *Gazelle,* an 8.15 ton, junk-rigged vessel carried: One 75 lb. fisherman with ⁵⁄₁₆″ chain and ⅝″ nylon, one 50 lb. fisherman and one 20 lb. four-prong grapnel.

Later, on *K'ung Fu-Tse,* 48′6″ long, he fitted: Two 125 lb. fisherman anchors, two 85 lb. Northills, one 75 lb. fisherman, one 50 lb. Northill and two 35 lb. grapnels.

On our own *Foudroyant,* a 32′ 6-ton ketch, we carry: One 35 lb. CQR with 100′ of ⁵⁄₁₆″ chain and 100′ of ⅝″ nylon, one 22 lb. Danforth with 40′ of ⁵⁄₁₆″ chain and 200′ of ½″ nylon, one 30 lb. fisherman with 100′ of ½″ nylon, and one 11 lb. Danforth for a stern anchor. We also carry 200′ of ⁹⁄₁₆″ Dacron for towing or kedging.

It has been said that you can judge a man's cruising experience by the quality of his ground tackle. The more experienced the skipper, the heavier will be his anchors and the better will be the gear for handling them. The above information seems to bear this out.

ANCHOR RODES

An anchor rode also may be called a line or a cable. Each term is equally correct.

WIRE

While wire is strong enough to serve as a rode (and if properly handled on a reel, it takes up very little space), it is rarely used on yachts. It has practically no shock-absorbing qualities and doesn't weigh enough to form a useful catenary. Wire also can be dangerous if improperly handled. A kink or tangle is very easy to achieve, very difficult to correct, and may result in permanently weakening the wire.

Hence wire generally is used in large yachts with room on the foredeck for a power winch and reel. Almost universally, rodes on yachts are either chain or rope—or a combination of the two.

ROPE

There are two suitable rope materials used for rodes, *nylon* three-strand and nylon braid. Two others are used occasionally and I will comment on them first just to dispose of the subject.

Dacron has adequate strength but has very low elasticity and is not considered suitable. Elasticity is a very important characteristic of an anchor rode. Dacron, however, has a place in your ground tackle. There may be times (as happens to the best of us) when it is necessary to kedge off during a grounding. The lack of elasticity is an asset when kedging.

67

Dacron is also the preferred material when towing or being towed.

Polypropylene is rarely used and for good reasons. It has no commendable characteristics when considered for this purpose, except perhaps low price. But what is your yacht worth? Only the best, not the cheapest!

Its characteristics are poor stretch, easy abrasion, readiness to hockle and, while some may select it because it floats and does not lie on the bottom where it may chafe, this is its most serious disadvantage.

On two occasions I witnessed trouble caused by this floating material. One sultry day in late summer we pulled into Annapolis and anchored in Spa Creek to wait out the thunderstorm that was brewing. When the squall hit, it was only moments before a small (unoccupied) cruising yacht went skittering across the narrow river, bow first and dragging its anchor.

Another skipper and I rowed over, set a second anchor and prevented any damage. The yacht had been anchored with polypropylene and as she swung in tide and breeze, the line had tangled around the rudder, cutting scope to a minimum. When the squall hit, the anchor quickly broke out.

On another occasion, a yacht was anchored on a quiet, calm Sunday afternoon when another yacht powered across her bow with what would normally be considered sufficient clearance. However, the floating polypropylene line was caught up and cut by the prop and the anchored yacht was cut adrift.

Of course, even *nylon* can be cut by the propellor of another boat. But at least nylon does not stay at the surface. This problem is completely eliminated by the use of chain. Hence, the only rope material suited for use as an anchor rode is nylon, which is both strong and elastic.

Should you use three-strand or braid, and what size should you select? Three strand has a greater elasticity than braid (25% for three strand, 14% for braid). Some consider this a disadvantage, as it acts as a rubber band. Danforth, undoubtedly the best known anchor manufacturer in America, recommends three strand. Samson, probably the best known rope manufacturer, recommends braid. Just another example of how the experts disagree on the important subject of anchors and equipment. Braid is easier to handle, it won't unlay, hockle or tangle, and is not too difficult to splice. However it is expensive, and in this sailor's opinion, the extra cost of braid over stranded rope for this purpose is not warranted.

Your calculations of anchor line strain for given wind strengths will tell you the minimum strength you need. Remember, most knots reduce the strength of the line by as much as 50%. Splices will retain about 70 to 90% of the line strength. Always use long splices.

Another point to consider is a line that is adequate for strength but very small in diameter will be harder on the hands. Also, deterioration due to abrasion, sunlight, or chafe will reduce the strength as time goes on. Select a line larger than indicated by the tables to ensure that, even after some deterioration, you still have a rode of adequate strength. It is good practice to limit working loads to $\frac{1}{5}$ the rated breaking strength of the rope. It also is very good practice to buy only the best. Be sure of what you are getting and don't buy what the store tells you is "just as good" and on sale this week. It's your yacht and your life that is at stake.

CHAIN

There are two general categories of chain used as anchor rodes, stud link and open link. Stud link is excellent but very difficult to find in the sizes we need and therefore is rarely used on yachts. We will concentrate our attention on the open link type. There are sufficient types of open link to meet all our needs.

The most common types of chain yachtsmen will encounter are *BBB, proof coil* and *high test*. They differ little in

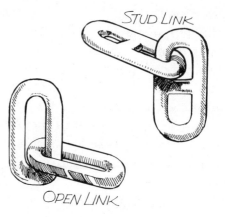

appearance, BBB having the shortest link, high test somewhat longer and proof coil the longest. If you are not an expert you probably won't recognize which type you are looking at.

However, when it comes to matching your chain and your windlass, the dimensions are of critical importance, for it may take one type readily but another will jump out of the pockets in the wildcat.

When ordering a wildcat, either buy the chain from the same source or send a sample of chain to the windlass supplier. Or, if you already have the windlass, get the manufacturer's instructions as to proper chain size to use.

A mismatch is both unsatisfactory and very dangerous. A chain running free on deck can cause serious injury and will quickly wear away or tear out the toerail.

The chain should be protected by hot-dip galvanizing. This is quite a different procedure from the bright electroplating you will see on chain at a hardware store. The latter will not last more than a day or so in saltwater. It is to be avoided entirely.

Even hot-dip galvanizing will wear off in time depending on the amount of use the chain gets and the care taken. The life of the chain can be prolonged by cleaning it with freshwater before stowing or by pulling it out of the locker, ranging it out on deck or on a dock when moored alongside and hosing it off.

When loss of galvanizing or other signs of wear exhibit themselves, the chain should be turned end-for-end.

The chain can be re-galvanized though this is a job for professionals. Each time the chain is heated, as it must be in the galvanizing process, some of the strength is lost. A competent and conscientious shop can do the job with minimum loss of strength, and it may, in fact, be done several times over a period of years before it must be replaced.

Painted chain or chain coated in plastic is not suitable for use by serious cruising folk. It may meet a need (in short lengths) for gunkholing, for it reduces rust stains on deck. In my experience, often more rust exists with plastic-coated chain than with hot-galvanized chain. How do you know how rusty the chain is under its plastic coating?

There are several definitions used by chain manufacturers that are important to us.

Working load limit is the maximum load in pounds that should ever be applied to the chain under any circumstances.

Proof test is the load applied to the chain during or after manufacture to detect defects. This is measured in pounds. If you deal directly with a chain manufacturer you should be able to get a certificate of proof test.

Minimum break test is the minimum load in pounds under which new chain has been found by experience to break.

The definition of most interest to us is the first, the working load limit, which usually is taken as ⅕ the minimum break test.

How much of a safety factor do you want in your rode? If you never expect to be caught out and forced to anchor in order to save the boat, perhaps a safety factor of 5:1 is too great. It's up to you to decide. Is saving a few dollars and a few extra pounds up forward a valid trade-off for the safety of you, your crew and your property? I'm sure Bill Rogan of *Watooka* would say NO!

The figures calculated earlier for your yacht should be used in determining the minimum size chain you need under the wind strength you used in the calculations.

In my own experience, many of the clerks in marine chandleries have no idea whatsoever concerning which type of chain is strongest. Rarely can they even identify the type they have in stock. Buy from a reputable dealer and get a certificate from the manufacturer.

If in any doubt, consider using a size larger or changing from BBB to high test. The latter is considerably stronger, will usually fit the same wildcat (verify this for yourself) but is more expensive.

The larger size will produce deeper catenary and therefore be a better shock absorber, reducing the jerks on chain, anchor and deck fittings.

It must be noted here that not all manufacturers use the same terminology (e.g. BBB, high-test). Whenever possible, get the manufacturer's ratings for the chain you plan on purchasing.

POLYESTER BRAID

A new material has come on the market recently. It is made in Sweden, called ANKAROLINA, and consists of polyester braid on a strong plastic reel.

The braid has good stretch characteristics and strength but the outstanding characteristic of this product is the ease of storing and the very compact storage reel.

Three sizes are available, No. 56 is rated at 5500 pounds breaking strength and comes with 168 feet on the reel; No. 24 has the same strength with 72 feet on the reel; No. 35 is rated at 3500 pounds and has 105 feet on the reel.

The reel is wound using a winch handle but it must not be used as an anchor windlass. It can be mounted almost anywhere convenient.

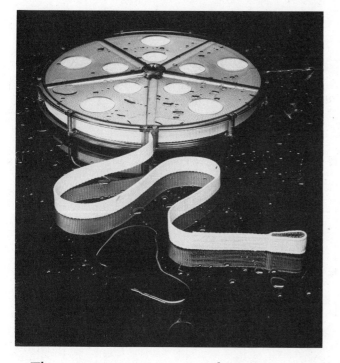

Polyester braid. Photo courtesy Geedon Marine Ltd.

The system seems to me to have some excellent possibilities. I haven't tried it and probably wouldn't consider it for main rode on my own yacht because it couldn't be used with my windlass. However, it would appear to be ideal for my stern anchor, with the reel attached to the stern pulpit or to the inside of a cockpit locker. The braid can be secured to a cleat in the same manner as rope.

RELATIVE ADVANTAGES OF ROPE AND CHAIN

Rope is subject to severe chafe, even parting, due to rubbing against debris or coral on the sea bottom and due to friction at the chock or hawse hole. It may last only a few minutes in heavy coral. Chain does not suffer in this respect and this is one of its greatest advantages.

Chain takes a much deeper catenary, permitting the actual pull on the anchor to be much nearer to horizontal, a very desirable feature. This can be accomplished with rope by

73

Campbell System Number	Size				Dimensions				Mechanical Properties				General Information	
	Trade Size		Actual Material Diameter		Inside Length		Inside Width		Working Load Limit		Proof Test (Minimum)		Approx. Weight Per 100 Feet	
	Inches	mm.	Inches	mm.	Inches	mm.	Inches	mm.	Pounds	Kg.	Pounds	Q.	Pounds	Kg.
3	1/8	4	.156	3.96	.89	22.61	.29	7.33	375	170	750	3.3	22	10
3	3/16	5	.218	5.53	.95	24.13	.40	10.16	750	340	1,500	6.7	41	19
3	1/4	7	.281	7.14	1.00	25.40	.50	12.70	1,250	567	2,500	11.1	72	33
3	5/16	8	.343	8.71	1.10	27.94	.50	12.70	1,900	862	3,800	16.9	106	48
3	3/8	10	.406	10.31	1.23	31.24	.62	15.75	2,650	1,200	5,300	23.6	155	70
3	7/16	11	.468	11.39	1.37	34.80	.75	19.05	3,500	1,590	7,000	31.1	217	98
3	1/2	13	.531	13.49	1.54	39.12	.79	20.07	4,500	2,040	9,000	40.0	270	122
3	5/8	16	.656	16.36	1.87	47.50	1.00	25.40	6,900	3,130	13,800	61.4	415	188
3	3/4	20	.781	19.34	2.12	53.85	1.12	28.45	9,750	4,420	19,500	86.7	577	262
3	7/8	22	.906	23.01	2.34	59.44	1.37	34.80	11,375	5,160	22,750	101.2	770	349
4	1/4	7	.281	7.14	.79	20.07	.40	10.16	2,600	1,180	4,300	19.1	80	36
4	5/16	8	.343	8.71	1.01	25.65	.48	12.19	3,900	1,770	6,700	29.8	111	50
4	3/8	10	.406	10.31	1.15	29.21	.58	14.73	5,400	2,450	8,900	39.6	160	73
4	7/16	11	.468	11.39	1.29	32.77	.67	17.02	7,200	3,270	11,900	52.9	216	98
4	1/2	13	.531	13.49	1.43	36.32	.76	19.30	9,200	4,170	15,300	68.1	280	127
4	5/8	16	.656	16.36	1.79	45.47	.90	22.86	11,500	5,220	19,500	86.7	413	187
4	3/4	20	.781	19.34	2.21	56.13	1.10	27.94	16,200	7,350	27,000	120.1	580	263
7	1/4	7	.281	7.14	.86	21.84	.45	11.43	3,150	1,430	6,700	29.8	75	34
7	5/16	8	.343	8.71	1.01	25.65	.48	11.68	4,700	2,130	9,400	41.8	111	50
7	3/8	10	.394	10.00	1.10	27.94	.55	13.97	6,600	2,990	13,200	58.7	150	68
7	7/16	11	.468	11.39	1.29	32.77	.67	17.02	8,750	3,970	17,500	77.8	212	96
7	1/2	13	.512	13.00	1.55	39.37	.72	18.29	11,300	5,130	22,600	100.5	238	108

This information was supplied by the Campbell Chain Division of the McGraw Edison Company.
System 3 is roughly comparable to what another manufacturer might designate Proof Coil.
System 4 might be referred to as High Test. Always get the manufacturer's specifications.

74

sliding a chum or riding weight down to near-bottom, though this adds complexity to the system.

Chain generally needs somewhat less scope to meet the same strain in windy conditions. This means your swinging circle will be much smaller, a very important advantage, indeed, when you must anchor amidst the crowd.

Rope generally is easier to handle, if you must handle it by hand. Obviously it also is much lighter. This lightness means less work if you pull it in by hand. However, those who use chain almost invariably use a windlass, which makes it even easier and safer to handle. The extra weight of the chain may appear to be a disadvantage but it adds to your holding power, which is a very great advantage.

Rope has elasticity, a very important feature in reducing snubbing. A chain has no elasticity and you have only to be caught anchored with short scope when a sea makes up to learn how severe this may be. It will feel as if the boat is being pulled apart each time the chain takes the strain. This can be prevented readily by adding some nylon in the rode, or by using another means of snubbing. These include spring and rubber mechanisms on deck (rarely seen except on the largest yachts) or by concocting your own snubbing system.

The most common solution is to attach a length (possibly two different lengths) of nylon to a deck cleat at one end, or to an eye in the stem of the yacht, and to the chain using a chain claw, chain hook or rolling hitch.

The chain then hangs down in a bight between the bow roller and the chain hook. The nylon takes the strain. Its elasticity reduces the severe snubbing but the chain is still secured just in case the nylon should part.

Chain is much more expensive than rope.

In my opinion, chain with a windlass generally is safer than rope. There is less chance of accidentally getting entangled and injured, or suffering rope burns. However, whenever you are working with heavy anchors on a heaving foredeck, you should take the utmost precautions.

Rope, while it may be stowed wet, should be cleaned as sand or rust between the fibers can cause abrasion. It must be flaked down so it will run freely the next time it is needed. This may necessitate having someone up in the forepeak making sure it is flaked down properly.

Chain certainly needs to be cleaned before stowing for it can bring up great quantities of foul-smelling mud. However, in a properly designed chain locker with short navel pipe, it is the simplest thing in the world to stow.

A rope, of course, is quiet. If you hear any squeaking, this means chafe, so get up there and put on some chafe-guard, and add a snubber.

The sound of chain dragging across a rocky bottom may keep you awake at night, at least until you get used to it. Learn to interpret the different sounds that a chain makes. It may warn you when the anchor starts to drag.

Read how author Stephen Dashew eased the assault on his ears while anchored with chain (*Yachting*, February 1982):

"To ease the strain, we rigged our standard double shock absorber. This consists of a 30′ piece of ⅜″ three-strand nylon tied to the chain with 6′ of chain slack, and a second section 8′ long with 2′ of chain slack. Normally the first section would be just stretched tight; in the big surges, the second would draw tight and occasionally the wildcat would take some load."

Rope deteriorates with sunlight, surface abrasion and hockles, along with internal abrasion from sand and rust. Chain deteriorates from rust and excessive strain. If the galvanizing gradually disappears, it can be replaced (by professionals) and unless the chain has been overstressed, it will be almost as good as new.

Both rope and chain should be checked from time to time and changed end-for-end whenever signs of wear or deterioration indicate a need.

It has been said that Americans prefer rope and Europeans prefer chain. This may be true of Americans who never leave their home waters. Almost universally, however, those who cruise extensively use chain principally, though perhaps not for the entire length.

COMBINING ROPE AND CHAIN

It is quite common, and proper practice, to use a length of chain attached to the anchor and a length of rope between chain and yacht. This provides the best features of both materials.

How long should each be? There exist no hard and fast rules, but you can't err by using more chain.

An all-chain rode may work satisfactorily much of the time but you must always be prepared to insert some shock-absorbing nylon into the rode.

When heavy wave action causes extensive sheering or snubbing, the severe shocks may cause trouble. Even in shallow water, the anchor may break out or some damage be caused.

In very deep water, such as when anchored in an open roadstead, it is best to have a high percentage of nylon. There is little advantage in having more than, say, 30 fathoms of chain, providing this is enough to ensure that the rope never touches coral or other debris.

For a small boat, less than 35 feet, I suggest 30 fathoms of chain for the main and secondary rode and nylon for the balance. Other rodes carried may be five fathoms of chain and the balance nylon. I suggest the minimum chain equal the boat length. One fathom of chain, as some carry, seems to me to serve little or no purpose.

You will note that the experts recommend more chain than I do, and Van Dorn goes further than most, recommending 54 fathoms of chain and 54 of rope.

Remember that the weak link in the system is most apt to be a point of attachment or joining—a knot, shackle or whatever. The finest rope and chain are useless if joined by an undersized shackle or a faulty knot.

FASTENING AND JOINING

Some yachtsmen will bend their line directly to the anchor ring using an *anchor bend* or a bowline with an extra turn around the ring. (See Figure Page 183). In both cases it is wise to seize the free end to the rode. Keep in mind that the knots reduce the strength of the line 40 to 50%.

A long eye splice with thimble in the end of the line, shackled to the anchor, is stronger. It only reduces line strength 10 to 15%. There are several important considerations here. Be sure to use many tucks for the splice. Be sure to secure the pin in the shackle with wire through the eye in the pin and around the inside of the shackle.

If you use a galvanized steel shackle, then use galvanized steel wire. If you use a stainless steel shackle, use stainless wire. Do not mix metals as corrosion will result.

Be sure the thimble is tight in the eye splice and is seized

A shackle pin should be seized with galvanized wire (if using a galvanized shackle). This seizing was done with linen cord only to show up better in the photo.

Seizing on a thimble to ensure that it does not come out when the eye is stretched under strain.

to the line. Should the thimble come out during strain, the line not only loses its protection but may, in fact, be cut by the edge of the thimble, rather than be protected by it.

An eye splice and shackle is an acceptable way of joining rope and chain. The joint will not pass over a wildcat, however, and rarely will it pass through the navel of a windlass or a deck fitting.

The best possible form of eye splice is described by Van Dorn. It requires a specially made thimble, machined from nylon or PVC (not a difficult job by any means). The groove should be deep enough to completely swallow the rope and its hole should be an easy sliding fit on the shackle pin.

A homemade PVC thimble.

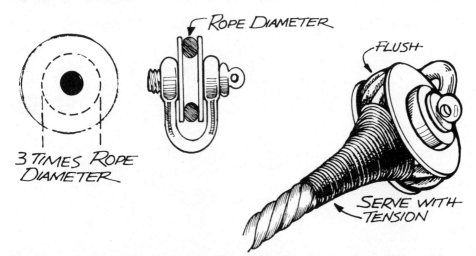

79

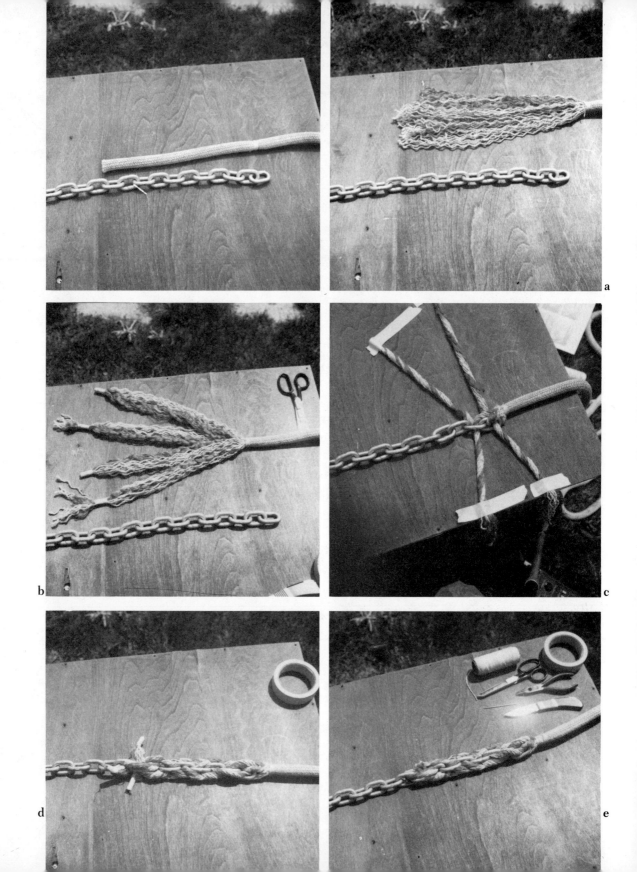

a

b

c

d

e

A rope-chain splice is not really difficult. The entire operation as shown took just 70 minutes including taking the pictures. The chain is ⁵/₁₆″ and the line is ⁵/₈″ braid. The rope must be unbraided and divided into four equal parts, each consisting of ¼ of the core and ¼ of the sheath. Three strand line must be treated similarly. Unlay the three strands and make up four equal bundles of thread.

The simplest to deal with is Marlow Multi-plait which is conveniently made up of eight strands and therefore easily divides into four parts.

(a) The rope should be whipped and then unravelled for a distance equal to twelve links of the chain. You will find that a certain amount of combing is necessary to keep the threads untangled. A fid will help with this.

(b) Divide the threads into four equal groups, pull them reasonably tight and twist slightly. Wrap some tape around the ends and trim off the rough ends outside the tapes. These operations will make the four parts easier to handle.

(c) This shows how the four parts go through the links of the chain. Do it a link at a time and keep the parts reasonably tight. I found that taping the parts down onto the table temporarily as I worked kept them organized and helped maintain tension.

(d) Continue the operation, link after link. Keep the parts as tight as you can. Tug the chain frequently. It helps keep the parts of the rope snug along the chain.

When you come to the end of the rope parts (with rope through 10 links) there will be two parts crossing one another in one link and the two other parts will cross one another in the adjacent link.

At each of these two "crossings" seize the two parts together very securely. I use linen whipping cord and a large sail needle to get into the cramped quarters. This seizing is important.

(e) Cut off the tips of the parts and melt them to prevent any unravelling. Now stretch, rope in one hand and chain in the other. A few strong tugs will help pull the parts of the rope in snugly against the chain.

Such a splice will pass over a rope-chain gypsy on your windlass quite readily.

Splice with six tucks, tapering the last two. Treat the tucked strands with silicone rubber to increase slip resistance. Put moderate tension on the finished splice, then serve with marline finishing up against the thimble.

A permanent chain-to-rope splice is much better and easier to handle. It has a rated strength of about 90% of the rope strength, providing it is well made. It removes the dangerous problem of having to lift a splice (eye-splice and shackle-to-chain) off a wildcat when under strain.

The catalog size of the shackle is usually slightly smaller than the diameter of the pin. However a ⅜" shackle will fit a ⅜" chain but does not have the same strength. It becomes the "weak link." Check the manufacturer's ratings. As with chain and rope, the safe working load is generally considered to be ⅕ its breaking strength. You may wish to select a larger shackle.

When swivels are fitted, which is rarely the case except on permanent moorings, use a larger size than you use for shackles. Swivels are frequently a weak link.

Whenever possible, get the manufacturer's ratings for shackles and swivels and be guided by them. The material included here was furnished by Wilcox Critenden.

If you must join two shots of chain, use a special chain shackle. This device is fitted with an oval (rather than round) pin and has no protrusions, so it will pass over most wildcats. The only source I have found for them is J. Stuart Haft of Bradenton, Florida.

There are "connecting links" available for permanently joining chain. With these it is necessary to peen over several rivets to make the link secure. Despite the manufacturer's claim that the link is as strong as proof chain, I much prefer to have one long, unbroken piece of chain.

Don't forget to secure the bitter end, otherwise you may experience the embarrassing and expensive sight of seeing your rode disappear forever over the bow.

It should be possible to cut the rode conveniently in an

emergency. If all chain is used, attach a short piece of line between the end of the chain and some strong point below-decks. The line should be long enough that it will come up on deck to be cut.

WHY ANCHORS BREAK OUT

Assuming your anchor is buried properly and is under reasonably steady strain, what will cause it to pull out and drag?

It may drag because the gravel, sand, mud, shell or silt has such poor cohesive quality there is really very little to restrain the anchor. It just pulls through as though it were embedded in pudding.

Even in hard sand or mud, sufficient horizontal force on the rode will pull the anchor forward somewhat, as a horse pulls a plow through the earth, though it may bury deeper until something gives up and breaks. At times the strain will be sufficient to bend, break or otherwise deform the anchor, causing it to release quickly. Or a link or a shackle may part. Thus the need for a strongly constructed anchor and a well-matched rode.

Should the boat swing and the pull come from a different direction, this too may cause the anchor to tip over and pull out. Sometimes it will reset itself in line with the new strain, and all is well.

When the pull is upwards, instead of horizontal, most anchors will tend to pull out. The steeper the angle, the quicker it will pull out. Some pull out more quickly than others as the scope ratio is reduced. This is why higher scope ratio is so important when we want security and why low scope ratio, i.e. 1:1, is employed when we want to pull the anchor out and weigh.

The load on your anchor rode is usually far from steady. Shock loads on the rode, whether from the wind or wave

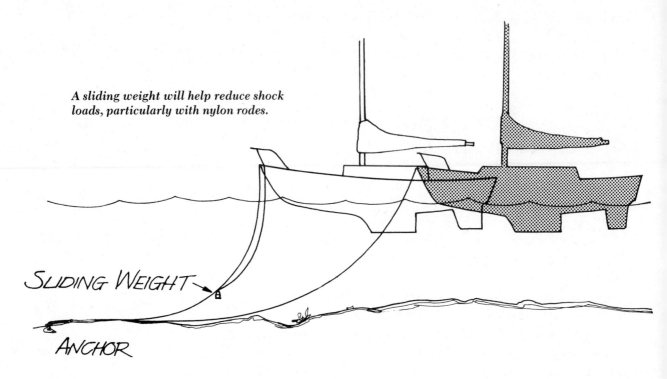

A sliding weight will help reduce shock loads, particularly with nylon rodes.

SLIDING WEIGHT

ANCHOR

action are a major cause of the anchor breaking out and a major cause of gear damage. Severe shock loads may be many times the steady strain on the rode.

Much can be done to reduce this shock load. The weight of a chain and the catenary it produces is some help. It should be noted however, that it does not take much strain to straighten out a catenary. Following that, all the strain comes on boat fittings and on the anchor. Sliding a weight down the rode to nearly touch the bottom is some help, particularly if the rode is of nylon.

Increasing the scope helps reduce snubbing but it is important to have some elasticity in the rode. The simplest way to accomplish this is to introduce nylon into the ground tackle system, either as part of the rode or as a snubber.

We've discussed previously in this chapter how to fashion a snubber.

It is advantageous to attach at least one snubber to a strong eye in the stem near the waterline. This reduces vertical height and therefore increases the scope ratio without increasing the swinging circle. It will also reduce the tendency of the boat to range about.

Nylon snubbers. (a) *takes the strain initially and snubber* (b) *is idle. As strain increases,* (b) *takes some strain. Should the snubbers part, the chain will still hold the boat secure.*

The snubbers should be a smaller size line than you would normally use for the rode. This increases elasticity, making them better shock absorbers. In the event a snubber should break, the chain will still hold your boat at anchor and give you time to take other precautions. You may want to "mouse" the chain hook so that it will not be lost in the event the snubber should break.

MARKING YOUR RODE

Whatever marking system you devise to know how much rode is payed out, keep it simple; a new crewmember should be able to recognize it readily—ideally without much explanation.

For nylon, the purpose-made plastic markers are convenient, though they don't last very long. For that matter, I haven't found anything that I would confidently call "long life."

First decide what units you want to identify. There is no need to mark every fathom, especially if you normally anchor in fairly deep water. Perhaps every three fathoms would be adequate, starting at the third and even going to every five after a considerable depth.

Use a marking material that will last reasonably long and is easy to replace. If your chain is permanently attached to the nylon, the marks should start with the chain, of course, and continue on to the nylon. You want to know the total rode in use.

John Mellor described this system in *Sail* in July, 1982. It seems like a good code, though you needn't use every mark. A piece of leather thong lasts reasonably well and is easy to work with.

You may mark your chain with the same code, though many sailors use a paint code. Leather, nylon cord or paint all will wear or chafe readily off chain, particularly if you

Fathoms	Marking
1	One knot in piece of thong
2	Two knots
3	Three knots
4	Four knots
5	Circular piece of leather
6	One knot plus circular leather
7–9	Additional knots plus leather circle
10	Leather circle with a hole in it
11	Ditto, plus one knot in thong
12–14	Etc. in sequence
15	Two pieces of leather, one circular the other with a hole in it
16	Two circles of leather, one with a hole, plus a thong with one knot
17–19	Etc. in sequence
20	Two circles of leather with holes in each

anchor in coral or rocks. You will have to touch up the paint or replace the marks fairly often.

For short lengths of chain, the simplest method is to paint the links as follows:

For first fathom, paint one link, 2 for the second, 3 for the third and so on up to 10. Paint every five fathoms thereafter repeating one link painted for 15 fathoms, 2 for 20 and so on.

An alternate code, quite easy to understand, involves painting three links at each point as follows:

Reading from the anchor end, the unpainted link between the first two painted is the number of 5-fathom units and those between the second two painted links is the number of 1-fathom units of chain out. For example,

This marking shows 1 link between first and second painted links, thus 5 fathoms. Also there are 3 unpainted links between second and third painted links, therefore 3 fathoms. Total: 8 fathoms.

5 + 3 = 8

TO ANCHOR

87

It is very important to have your rode marked in some such manner, so that it can be read easily, day or night.

You may be called up in the night with a feeling that you should veer more rode. How much is already out? How much still is in the locker? Did one of the crew veer more before going to bed? The marks will tell.

ADDITIONAL GROUND TACKLE ELEMENTS

RIDING WEIGHT

It is advisable to carry a weight which can be slid down the rode to back the anchor. This helps keep the pull on the anchor in a horizontal direction, which reduces the danger of pulling it out. It also helps decrease objectionable snubbing by wind and waves. The severe, jerky strains will not be felt by the stem, nor by the anchor, until the rode is stretched almost straight.

If lowered right to the bottom so that it drags, a weight can reduce objectionable sheering very effectively. In fact, the weight always should be lowered to the bottom for best effect. Halfway down is not nearly so effective.

The weight sometimes is attached to the rode with a large shackle. This is satisfactory with chain, but is apt to cause

A purpose-made traveller for a sentinel.

88

chafe on a nylon rode. For rope, a proper traveller should be employed.

A light line should be attached to the traveller with which you may lower and raise the weight.

What kind of weight and how much? I carry a 30 lb. weight made of steel plates. Sometimes it seems too much. Carry different weights if this is practical. If not, then try approximately the same weight as your best bower. Some use a piece of chain, tied up in a bundle, or carried in a canvas bag. Others use a spare anchor. Many possibilities exist. See figure, page 8.

CHAFE PREVENTERS

Ropes passing over the bow roller or through chocks or hawse holes always are subject to chafe. You should carry something to reduce this danger. There are purpose-made chafe-guards, but pieces of rubber hose, leather, patio carpet, even heavy cloth such as canvas will work satisfactorily.

Plastic garden hose looks good but will not last long. Rubber hose, such as you may find in an automotive parts shop, is much better. If possible, feed the line through the hose without slitting it. If you must slit the hose, make sure the solid side rather than the slit side is against the spot where

Purpose-made chafe guard.

chafe occurs. Fasten the hose in place with hose clamps or heavy seizing. See figure, bottom page 10.

Be sure to protect the rode from chafe against the bobstay. A long piece of hose may help here but using a snubber to an eye in the stem solves this problem completely.

In a gale, like it or not, you should go forward frequently and, if indicated, replace the chafe-guard and freshen the nip.

Patience Wales, managing editor of *Sail*, wrote some years ago about *Kismet*, which was forced to anchor behind an island in the Red Sea to weather a storm that lasted nine days. Two rodes chafed through despite their best efforts. Two anchors with chain were lost, though one was found later by diving with mask and flippers.

SOUNDING LEAD

This is a valuable tool to help you select your anchorage. Your echo sounder may be able to tell you the depth of the water but rarely informs you accurately about bottom material. A lead can. It is fitted with a recess in the bottom, which traditionally is "armed" with tallow. Lacking tallow, you will find peanut butter will work. Lower the lead to the bottom gently and bring it up again for inspection. Samples of sand, mud, shells or whatever will be stuck in the tallow, giving you an indication of what lies under you. Also, in moderate depths, you can feel, in the line, whether the lead strikes soft or hard material on the bottom.

The skill of the old-timer in swinging the lead and reading the bottom from what he found on the tallow is another of those skills largely lost to us today.

Surgeon Rear Admiral John Muir, in his book, *Messing About In Boats* (Blackie & Son Ltd., Glasgow, 1938) tells of his early days, circa 1910, on a "sailing ship missioning to the North Sea fishing fleet." He wrote, "Their method of navigation was simple, and entirely the fruits of experience.

When in doubt as to their position they took a cast of the lead, considered the depth, looked at the arming carefully, smelt it and then rubbed their tongue over it. The latter process gave them an idea of the coarseness of the bottom sand, and was the only way they could gauge it as their hands were not sensitive enough. With a little thought they could give the position to within a mile or so, and there was rarely any error in the statement."

Even if you have a good electronic sounder, be sure to carry a lead as well.

THE DINGHY

At times you may want to set a second (or third) anchor out, and in certain circumstances this can best be done with the dinghy. It has long been argued whether or not an inflatable is suitable. In moderate weather perhaps it is. Personally, I find a hard dinghy far better in rough water or if you have any distance to row. I also find my dinghy very handy for rounding up my anchors (using trip lines) after conditions have indicated more than one was desirable. While the yacht continues to ride to one anchor, the others may be gathered in without disturbing anyone, even the other boats that have swung over my anchors.

DIVING GEAR

Whenever possible and practical it is highly desirable to sight your anchor to ensure it has actually buried properly. This may be done from the dinghy using a glass-bottom bucket, assuming the water is clear and not too deep, of course.

It can be done better, and more enjoyably in many cases, by going over the side with flippers and mask. You can learn in situ about how your ground tackle works.

On occasion I have found my snorkel gear invaluable when

It is frequently good practice to dive and ensure that the anchor is digging in properly.

an anchor or chain became tangled or fouled in coral. In severe cases, you will find Scuba gear well worthwhile. Such gear also can save you hundreds of dollars if otherwise the anchor and chain must be slipped and lost (or already has done so).

ANCHOR BUOYS

It frequently is advisable to buoy your anchor. This shows others (as well as yourself) just where your anchor is located and will help reserve your swinging room. It is particularly important when you must set two or more anchors. Anchor buoy lines, when attached to the anchor crown, also serve to help trip deeply buried anchors.

92

Almost any conspicuous floating object can be used as a buoy. Frequently, small fenders or white plastic containers are employed. You may like to put the name of your vessel on it and also mark it "anchor buoy." This will help reduce the danger of it being mistaken for a mooring buoy or a lobster pot.

Your buoy line, or trip line, should be just long enough to reach the foredeck at high tide. Too much line will permit the buoy to drift out of place, defeating its purpose. Further, it increases the danger of fouling the prop or rudder of other boats that may come too close.

The trip line should be ⅜" in diameter or larger. Anything smaller may prove impractical if the anchor is particularly difficult to pull out backwards. Dacron is better than nylon for this purpose.

When weighing, be careful the buoy line does not drift back and foul your own prop. Pull the buoy up onto the deck when you start to lift the anchor and keep the slack buoy line that remains in the water to a minimum. The same applies to slack anchor line. Pull in as much as possible before tripping the anchor.

The actions of your anchor buoy sometimes will tell you if your anchor is dragging. Keep an eye on it after you anchor

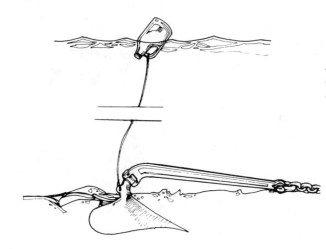

An anchor is buoyed by attaching a trip-line between its crown and a small buoy on the surface.

and see whether or not it appears to lie still and stay in the same place. Don't be fooled by current or tide movement past the buoy.

There is no need to use a very large anchor buoy. Remember, its purposes are to mark your anchor's position, to provide a trip line and to reduce the danger of others anchoring too close. I've never found it to be too effective in fulfilling this last purpose. More than once, when I've been ready to weigh, I've been forced to ask the other yacht to pull in some of his rode so I could get my anchor up.

Too large a buoy is too attractive to the landlubber who wants to moor to it, thus lifting your anchor out and setting you drifting into other yachts or out to sea.

An alternative to buoying (for the purpose of later tripping the anchor) is to becue the anchor. Becueing involves securing the rode to the crown and lashing it to the shank with light line. In setting the anchor, the strain is along the shank and the anchor sets normally.

A CQR becued. The chain is shackled to the crown and lashed to the ring with light line or wire. Putting strain on the rode from above will break the lashing and permit the anchor to be pulled out backwards.

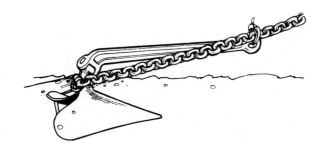

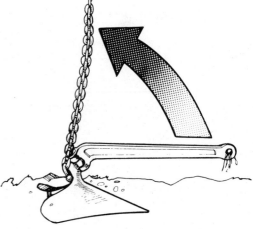

When it comes to breaking it out, the strain on the short rode breaks the light becueing line and the anchor is hauled out crown first.

At least that is the theory. I expect it works, but what happens should your yacht swing through, say 45° or more? The light line would break if the strain is at all severe and the anchor, with the rode attached to the crown, could now pull out.

I don't like the idea of becueing an anchor unless you can be sure you won't swing, as for example, when anchored in a steady current, or for a short period only. An anchor watch is advised.

LIGHTS AND SHAPES

By all laws of good seamanship, you are required to indicate to other yachtsmen and commercial operators that you are at anchor, if the area is frequented by other yachts and boats. (The exception is designated anchorage areas.)

Between sunset and sunrise, the proper way is to show a white light all around. Two common ways of doing this are with a masthead light or by a lantern or electric light hung in the rigging. Small battery-operated lights are available that are controlled by photocell and turn themselves on and off automatically.

While a masthead light is convenient, I prefer a light nearer to deck level. Personally, when I must maneuver around after dark, I'm more apt to be looking at deck level, not up in the sky. I expect most others are the same.

When anchored in daylight you are required to show a spherical black shape in the rigging. This is supposed to be 0.6 m (2′) in diameter. You rarely see them, but that is only because many of us are negligent in this matter.

In fog, if near a channel, don't forget to sound your bell for about five seconds each minute. Better by far to anchor well out of any channel.

DECK GEAR

Bitts, Samson posts, cleats and chocks help fasten the rode and the mooring lines. Samson posts or bitts were ideal in their day. They were oaken beams fitted right through the deck to the keel and would hold any strain that might be put on them. Not only were they fitted up on the foredeck but frequently also in each quarter.

One would be lucky to find one vessel in a hundred produced today fitted with Samson posts or bitts.

In fact many do not even have cleats fore and aft and those that one does see fitted are often mere toys, suitable for tying up in a quiet marina while skipper and guests are aboard, enjoying their drinks. A good cleat must be large enough to handle large-diameter rodes and mooring lines and must be fastened through a backing plate to prevent them from being ripped through the deck.

The same with hawse holes in the bulwarks. What is a bulwark, you ask? It is a continuation of the hull above the sheer line, or planking around the upper deck. It stops the seas from boarding and prevents the crew from being swept overboard in high seas.

Hawse holes generally have gone the way of the dodo, with good chocks now taking their place.

Every boat worthy of being taken out of harbor should be fitted with something to take the place of bitts, forward, amidships and aft. Cleats usually are used nowadays and instead of hawse holes, chocks or fairleads should be fitted.

The cleats should be large enough and heavy enough to take two or more turns of the largest rope you could ever be expected to handle, at anchor, at dockside, or being towed. Similarly the chocks should take the same size rope with plenty of room to spare for chafe-guard. On a 30-footer, 1″ is the minimum, on a 45-footer, 1½″ and so on.

Mid-ship chock and cleat make rigging spring lines fore and aft a very simple operation.

Cleats and chocks *must* be smooth and well faired. Chocks particularly, which are frequently cast aluminum alloy, may have sharp edges inside the opening. Such edges can cut through a nylon line under strain in a matter of minutes. I prefer closed chocks, though open ones are seen more frequently. The lines will often be pulled out of an open chock when tied up alongside in a tidal slip.

If you don't already have good cleats and chocks, three of each to port and three more to starboard, give serious thought to adding more. When you do, be sure to use heavy, stainless steel bolts and backing plates to spread the load under the deck. Bed them in well to prevent any leaks.

An excellent bronze Samson post mounted on the quarter of this fine yacht.

97

THE WINDLASS AND OTHER FOREDECK FIXTURES

I would not say that a windlass is essential on any cruising boat but it certainly goes a long way towards making cruising, anchoring and weighing far more pleasant. It can eliminate much of the back-straining, hernia-inducing work associated with anchoring and certainly makes it possible for every adult crewmember, no matter how small, to handle the anchor with relative ease. Please note I prefer to handle the anchor while my mate stays in the cockpit, attending to the helm, the engine, and so on.

Even a small manual windlass will multiply anyone's muscle power by about 10. Hauling up 150 pounds of anchor and chain only requires 15 pounds of pull and push on the windlass handle.

Electric and hydraulic windlasses also are available. Should you fit one of the latter two types, make sure it can be operated efficiently by hand should the mechanism fail. The advantage of a powered windlass is the much greater ease of handling your gear and therefore the tendency to use heavier tackle.

Most, if not all, windlasses are fitted with a clutch and brake making it easy to check the rode as it is being veered

A heavy-duty, electric windlass with bollard on top.

and to hold it when you have let out all you want out. Some also are fitted with a pawl or dog to hold the wildcat in place. This never should be relied on to take the severe strain of the anchor. Never let the windlass be subjected to severe snubbing. Its gears are not designed for this type of load. Use a chain stopper or snubber to protect it. The purpose of the pawl is to lock the wildcat temporarily, with one rode out, so you can still use the windlass gypsy to haul in a second anchor using a rope rode.

Usually the windlass is fitted with a chain stripper and a navel so the chain or rope will leave the wildcat easily and disappear directly through the deck to the locker down below, reducing deck clutter.

I am aware of only one advantage of a capstan over a windlass. That is that the pull can be taken to either side, whereas the windlass must take it from forward only. When it is necessary to kedge your boat off a sandbar, being able to pull directly to a kedge set off to port or to starboard can be a great help.

The powered units are wonderful. You can raise or lower your anchor from the cockpit if you wish, though I strongly recommend it be done from forward where you can see what is going on. You are dealing with a great deal of power and a slip or tangle could cause very serious damage.

If electric, be sure you have adequate power available, an extra large, well-charged battery bank and heavy electric cables—plus a circuit breaker in the line. Even then, it may be necessary to run the engine to supply charging power while raising the anchor.

Keep this equipment well maintained. More than one yacht has been set on fire by overloading the cables to the capstan. David Parker, in his excellent book, *Ocean Voyaging* (John De Graff, Inc., 1975), wrote, "I once used an electric winch on another yacht, on which I was crewing, to lift a plow anchor and 300' of heavy chain. Being not terribly bright, most of the crew were forward watching the operation. Imagine our surprise when we looked aft and found the yacht on fire! The electric cables had been too small for the current load and had become so hot that they set the engine room on fire."

He goes on to offer some good advice about the windlass switch. "The location of the windlass switch is sometimes critical because of the inherent danger of automatic devices. The foot, or step switch is dangerous if there is a chop running. The forward section of the yacht is narrow, and having just come in from the sea you will be somewhat unsteady in the new motion. It is easy to stumble and accidentally trip the switch. I know of more than one loss of legs from this kind of accident. A hand switch of the solenoid type with a master switch aft is perhaps the best combination for safety. I, for one, will never forget the picture of a man sitting on the foredeck staring incredulously at his leg lying on the opposite side of the yacht after tripping a foot switch and getting tangled in the rapidly moving chain."

Windlass and anchor installation on Foudroyant.

A hydraulic windlass eliminates the fire problem but requires more complicated gear and a hydraulic pump driven by the engine, which means the engine *must* be running in order to operate the windlass. This could mean there is no mechanical means of weighing anchor if the engine will not run. Another reason to keep it simple!

I have had a manual Simpson-Lawrence aluminum windlass on my boat for more than 10 years and it has never given me a bit of trouble. Some skippers prefer bronze because they believe corrosion is less of a problem.

In dire emergency, you may be able to haul in the anchor by taking a line from the rode, (a chain hook is handy here), back to a sheet winch or a halyard winch at the mast. Alternately, a handy-billy or some other block and tackle arrangement could do the job. None will work as well as a power windlass, of course, or even a manual windlass.

Bow rollers and chain lockers have been mentioned earlier. A proper bow roller, at the stem or at the end of a short bowsprit or at the side of a longer one, can be a real asset and a great convenience.

Both the roller and the bowsprit must be very strong to withstand the severe snubbing that results from strong wave action.

Even in calm weather, if your anchor is fouled or well dug in, the strain when pulling it out can be extreme. Some very poor bow roller assemblies exist on the market, intended to be attached after you have bought the boat. Also, some of the equipment builders incorporate into the boat during manufacture is ridiculously flimsy and unsuitable.

I've seen several bow rollers bent, broken and, on the foredeck of one boat, ripped off due to poor construction.

They must be strong! Larry and Lin Pardey called the Cabo San Lucas fiasco "The Ultimate Gear Test" (*Sail*, June, 1983) and wrote, "without a doubt, bow rollers were one of the weakest links in the anchoring systems." Remember, they are referring to boats used for extended cruising, not daysailing.

Examples of good bow roller design. I have found no "perfect" bow roller. These are good but all fall short in one way or another.

Poor bow roller and windlass
installation. The bow roller is
cantilevered excessively. It was soon
broken off taking some of the deck
with it. The windlass, although a
perfectly good Simpson-Lawrence
type, cannot be used properly as the
chain fouls with the forestay and
roller furling gear.

103

The roller must be capable of taking side loads, must be able to take such strains without chafing the rode, and must have some means of securing the rode so it cannot jump out.

Almost certainly, bow rollers must be custom built. There is very little of any value in the marine catalogs. If you are going to have one built, make it extra strong. Welded stainless steel ¼″ thick is none too strong for a 40′ boat. A good roller will be of stainless steel, nylon, or naval bronze, 4 to 6″ in diameter, and will have a shaft at least ¾″ in diameter. The roller will have a track machined to fit your chain as well as your line. It will be well faired with no rough or sharp edges and it will be a fairly close fit in the frame so there is no room for any line to get between the roller and the frame. Grease fittings should be incorporated.

The navel or deck opening must be large enough to eliminate any tendency for links to jam as they fall through or are pulled up. It should not be large enough to pass a harp shackle unless there is some ready and sure way of really closing this opening while at sea. A great deal of water can get below via the navel when green water sweeps the deck.

The chain should have a free fall at least 18″ from deck to

A brake and dog permit chain to be controlled and locked.

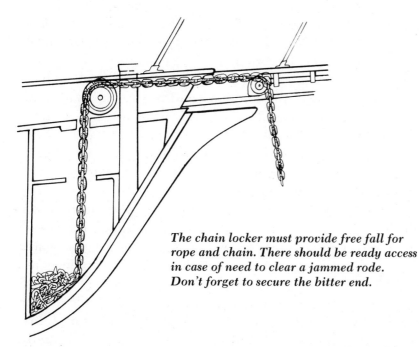

The chain locker must provide free fall for rope and chain. There should be ready access in case of need to clear a jammed rode. Don't forget to secure the bitter end.

the top of the pile. It may be allowed to pile up in a cone as it falls. The pile will collapse and generally this does not create a tangle.

There should, of course, be ready access to the chain locker in the forepeak. No matter what precautions you take, you cannot guarantee the perverse chain will not jam.

Rope is even more cantankerous. The rope locker should be well ventilated and accessible. All lockers should be well drained.

Do not use a chain pipe with rope if you can avoid it. Have as great a free fall as possible.

Consider partitioning the forepeak to permit stowing two separate rodes without tangling. Two navels are needed if you do this.

The foredeck must be reinforced before attaching all this gear, windlass, heavy cleats and the like. Many stock boats, built for the mass market, are intended for racing or coastal cruising and are not adequately reinforced. Boats designed

105

and built for extended offshore cruising usually are adequately strong, with reinforced foredecks and are capable of surviving extreme conditions without damage.

I suggest, as a minimum, reinforcing the foredeck with ½″ plywood under each item, plus—and this is important reinforcement for the windlass—crossbeams from side to side, right out to the gunwales.

On my 32′ boat, I added a piece of ½″ ply, triangular in shape, covering the entire forepeak roof and through which I bolted the windlass and cleats.

A very handy item up in the bows is a washdown pump. It will pay for itself when weighing and hauling in chain covered with foul-smelling slime. A bucket on a lanyard will serve, of course, though not with the same convenience and finesse.

Sometimes your anchor comes up completely hidden with great gobs of weed and mud. A large galley knife is useful or, best of all, a broad-bladed machete.

CHAPTER 3

Proper Anchoring Techniques

WORST CASES

Ninety-nine times out of a hundred cruising yachtsmen will be seeking some quiet, protected cove or harbor, with palm-shaded sandy beaches or pine and birch bejeweled granite walls, and with trout or grouper lurking in the depths.

That remaining 1% of the time, you may be caught out where you had no intention of being. That's the time when all your anchoring skills and systems will be sorely tested.

I'll never forget the tragic story a few years back concerning an elderly Southern California couple. Retirement time had arrived. They had sold all, bought a yacht and set off on that cruise of which he (at least) had been dreaming for years.

I'm sure it wasn't as casual as all that but, in any event, not many days later, they were coasting Baja California, both apparently seasick and the yacht out of control even though the weather was not unusual. Rather than staying well offshore, they were caught in the breakers. Soon their new home was washed ashore and totally wrecked. The couple survived but their savings were lost and their dream had evaporated.

Why had they not let out an anchor, with all possible rode? They could have been held far enough offshore to be safe, even if uncomfortable. They would have been out of the surf, out of immediate danger and could have waited for help to come or for the mal de mer to lessen so they could carry on. Anchoring off a lee shore is rarely a pleasant situation but it can save the day when few alternatives exist.

The records are full of cases of yachts lost when timely anchoring could have saved them. Many boats, of course, have been saved by lee shore anchoring.

If you must do it, anchor as far out as possible. The action of heavy swells is far less severe than that of breaking surf. If your rode will not reach bottom, leave it out anyway. As you approach shallower water, usually a 300 to 500′ rode will catch before you are in the surf. Of course, if a steep-to shore is in your lee even this technique may not save you.

Of all the sailors who ever have walked a quarter deck or risked their yacht to the sea's whims, Fred Fenger is among the luckiest. Read "The Cruise Of The *Diablesse*" published by *Yachting* in 1926. It's a classic!

Fenger had lived 3½ years on *Diablesse* (she devil) when he wrote this book. *Diablesse* was a wooden schooner, 52′ on deck and modeled after the Gloucester fishermen. He bought her down east and, with his wife and generally with a single native crew, they sailed throughout the Caribbean.

They were heading north in Exuma Sound and all were bone-tired from "pumping and eating and drinking our way to Nassau." We pick up the story as they spotted the Beacon

Waves get steeper as they approach a gradually sloping beach. A yacht anchored at (a) *will be very uncomfortable but relatively safe. The yacht at* (b) *would likely snatch its anchor out and drag ashore. Once in the surf it is very difficult to save a yacht.*

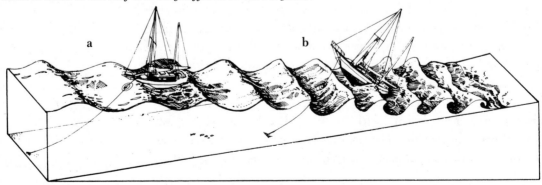

Cay light marking the entrance to the passage across the coral-studded Yellow Bank off Nassau.

"At four (a.m.) we hove to, well to weather of the entrance to Ship Channel—for we'd be waiting the light o'day for running through the reef.

"Then we pumped her dry and the skipper turned in below while the native crew stretched out his weary length in the cockpit. We'd snooze for an hour and by the time we had dried the ship again we would be able to see our way in, to the banks. But la, we slept like cherubs in the clouds, and nearly two hours had gone by when the rattle of the main-sheet block aclumping along the traveller brought us up all standing. The skipper landed in 4″ of water and fell up the companionway. Fred was already at the pump, yelling, 'Hey b'low, hey b'low, we gone t'rough.'

"And so we had, while the ship was on her ways to foundering! Nothing but empty seas astern where the cays should be all strung out in the morning light. To weather stood Beacon Cay, still blinking, while the seas were breaking wickedly on the reef. The entrance lay right off the tip of our bowsprit and the *Diablesse* had come through stern first, as safely as though we, ourselves, had brought her in. It was the current set up by the gale, which we had underrated, and had it not ranged her into the wind while sweeping her through the channel, we might have kept on sleeping till the high tide from our leak would have washed us off our berths, somewhere down on the Yellow Bank."

Don't count on that kind of luck! In similar circumstances, if it is impossible to man a watch all night, let out your anchor and a long rode. It could save you from disaster.

There may be times when you are obliged to anchor offshore. Perhaps there is no protected harbor handy. Possibly you need only a temporary lee of an island, a coral reef or a sandbar to sit out a bad blow.

Or you may simply want to wait for a tide change. The wind has dropped, the engine is out of order and the tide is against you. Why drift in the wrong direction? Anchor and wait for a change.

Hilaire Belloc in "The Cruise of the *Nona*" (1925) was returning home after a sail around Britain. His *Nona* was without engine and he was becalmed within sight of his home port but had a foul tide pushing him back out to sea.

"There were others in the same plight under the warm summer sky of that evening; a London barge, a Norwegian ship with timber, a little snorting steamer, which let go her anchor in a rush somewhere further out just at the moment when we dropped anchor in that very shallow water, in not five fathoms deep. A great full moon rose up out of the east, out of the seas of England, and the night was warm. There was a sort of holiness about that air. I was even glad that we had thus to lie outside under such a calm and softly radiant sky, with its few stars paling before their queen."

There are many remote islands and even some spots neither remote nor islands, where there is little or no protection offered to boats or even to ships waiting to unload their cargo into lighters.

These almost always are in a lee. But everywhere the wind is apt to change. If you must anchor off, set an anchor watch. Certainly don't leave the boat unattended for any prolonged time.

Sometimes the ground will be so steep in the lee of an atoll that, while you can put a chain around a coral hump up forward (or even tie to a tree ashore) and fall back a few feet for safety in deeper water, your longest rode will not touch bottom off the stern. This is a very precarious position, indeed, and never to be recommended. But if you must, leave that long rope and heavy anchor off the stern anyway. It might just save you should the wind or current shift.

Anchoring in the lee of an island for a short period to gain respite from a storm is quite common and is good seamanship, providing there is a watch kept by a capable crew. It likely will turn out to be very rough, even uncomfortable, for

Even when your stern anchor will not touch bottom, keep it out. Should the wind shift, it could keep you from dragging ashore.

the rollers may hit you at a different angle to the wind. You sometimes can reduce this by putting out a second anchor off the stern, or attaching a spring line from rode to quarter cleat to hold the boat near to right angles to the rollers, rather than at right angles to the wind. I've rarely found this to be entirely satisfactory, but it does help.

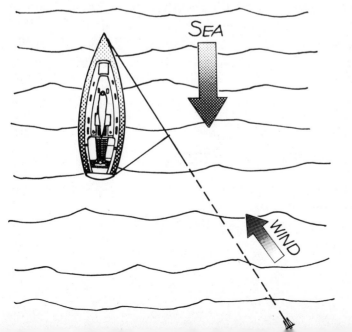

Use of a spring line or bridle when wind and sea conflict. The yacht may be turned so the bow heads in to the seas, thus reducing the rolling and discomfort.

111

And when you find yourself beset by heavy fog, when you are not sure where you are nor what hazards may be in your way, anchoring may be the best solution.

I recall reading of a court of enquiry that took place long ago, concerning an officer accused of "stranding and hazarding" one of Her Majesty's (that would be Queen Victoria) ships in a fog. He was only asked two questions by the president of the court, but they damned him for life.

"When the fog came in so thickly that navigation was attended with danger, were you in anchorage waters?"

"Yes."

"Why did you not anchor?"

No reply that would have satisfied a seaman was possible and the officer knew this and made no effort at any excuse. (From *Messing About In Boats* by J. R. Muir, Blackie & Son Ltd., Glasgow, 1938.)

DESIRABLE ANCHORAGE CHARACTERISTICS

As they say in the instructions for making proper chicken soup, first find a chicken. So, before we can practice anchoring, we first must find a place to anchor.

Everyone's idea of the ideal anchorage is not the same. Some prefer solitude, some crowds. Some want the noisy amenities of society, or access to overland transportation.

Long in advance you will have studied your charts, chartlet or cruising guides and decided what harbors offer those qualities you most enjoy. For the most part, any suitable anchorage will include:

1. Protection from wind and waves
2. Suitable depth
3. Suitable bottom
4. Friendly shores
5. Swinging room

6. Ease of escape

7. No insects or other nuisances

8. Traffic and other attractions and distractions

Let's look at them one by one.

AVOIDING WIND AND WAVES

Protection from strong wind and waves usually is obtained by anchoring in the lee of land. Occasionally you may have to be satisfied with protection from waves only, such as when you anchor in the lee of a sandbar or coral reef. Take into account the tide as this minimum shelter may be several feet underwater at high tide, changing conditions drastically.

You also may find that protection from wind does not always imply protection from waves, for the latter have a nasty habit of rolling around points into anchorages.

Give consideration early to how the situation will change should the wind shift. Will it still be a good anchorage? Remember Cabo San Lucas.

SUITABLE DEPTH

An anchorage that is too shallow may put you on the bottom with even minor condition changes. A falling tide may put your craft over on its side, which makes for difficult—if not dangerous—living. You should try to have at least 2' of water under the keel at low tide, everywhere in your swinging circle. So you must take the care to discover the bottom depth all around your anchor. Don't assume a regular bottom just because it's flat and sandy where you dropped anchor.

An anchorage that is too deep will make it more difficult to set suitable scope ratio, to sight the anchor, to haul in the ground tackle and perhaps to retrieve a fouled anchor. However there may be times when you must anchor in depths of 200', even more, especially if you cruise the south seas.

SUITABLE BOTTOM

This implies a bottom that is both good holding and free of hazards and obstructions. It also implies a reasonably level bottom, or at least, if grossly uneven, knowledge of the fact.

Your charts will probably tell you something about the bottom but frequently the information is out of date, in error or inadequate. Use your lead to check both the depth and bottom material. Check for hazards as well as abrupt changes in depth.

Best among holding materials is heavy sand. Worst are heavy weed, very light mud or silt, or gravel. However, providing you have a good selection of anchors and rodes, you can anchor in *almost* anything.

I say almost, because situations do exist that defy secure anchoring. They range from extremes of thoroughly scoured sand to hard limestone, shale or equivalent.

I've tried to anchor in a river mouth up north, where the combination of silt, sawdust and bark (from an old sawmill) had the consistency of thick pudding. Neither fisherman nor plow would hold. Mushroom anchors are ideal in this situation, but few pleasure craft carry them for they are heavy, awkward and from heavy mud often are impossible to retrieve.

At the other extreme, I'll not forget trying to anchor in a tidal creek at the southwest tip of Cat Island in the Bahamas.

Hawksnest Creek is a well protected, secluded anchorage, with mangroves both sides and a minimum depth of 6'. There is a beautiful beach nearby, also an airstrip, club, dining room and lounge. In all, it seemed an ideal spot to spend an evening after a day of sailing across Exuma Sound.

The bottom is hard, smooth limestone, almost as hard and smooth, in fact, as a concrete highway. Our fisherman just pulled across this slab and couldn't find a crack anywhere to hook onto. Our crew quickly nicknamed the anchorage the Hawksnest Drag Strip.

We ended up with lines across to the mangroves on both sides of the creek, brought to the bow. It worked fine and kept us secure and quiet all night, quiet that is, except for the swarms of sand flies that found us at dusk and were a real problem for an hour, at which time they disappeared just as suddenly as they arrived.

One feature attraction of this anchorage, which didn't get into the cruising guide, was the heavy concentration of photoluminescent creatures in the water. A bucket of water dipped from the creek and poured back in was a spectacular fireworks display. It was worth putting up with the flies!

A bottom that has abrupt changes in depth may create anchoring problems. You may find a shoal or other hazard within your swinging circle. Remember, shoals can be safe or hazardous depending on the state of the tide and wave action.

Alternatively, you can anchor near the edge of a dropoff, and you are safe as long as the wind blows you towards the shallower waters and your anchor holds. But if it shifts and blows you toward deeper water, a pulled anchor will have greater difficulty resetting itself and you may find yourself drifting out to sea. It happens not infrequently.

Anchoring with a hook in rocks, shale, shells or coral, is problematic, although in some cases it is necessary. Be aware of the dangers.

Your SAV, grapnel or fisherman may be hooked among some rocks and all the pulling you can provide by backing down full power will not dislodge it. It seems perfectly secure. You retire, only to be awakened in the night as wind and waves pick up and you realize you are dragging. What happened? The extra strain plus snubbing moved the rock slightly and the anchor pulled free.

Coral is even worse. It can be as hard as concrete but brittle as fine china. You may be hooked securely between the arms of some stag coral but if a squall hits, not only will you break off some of these antlers, possibly freeing the anchor,

115

but the chain ranging about down there may cause a lot of unnecessary ecological damage by breaking off entire coral heads. Also, your chain may become badly tangled among the coral as the boat sheered and swung about, that it will take many hours of diving with Scuba gear to clear it.

Of course, these problems won't be as severe if you use rope instead of chain. But in only a few minutes your rope can chafe through on coral and you will find yourself cut free and drifting, minus an expensive anchor.

When you don't have any idea what the bottom consists of, try using two anchors in tandem, one a burying type such as a CQR and the other a fisherman. It will double the chance of holding regardless of bottom. Connect your CQR to a chain rode, then fasten about 10′ of chain to the eye in the crown of the CQR and put the fisherman at the end of this.

FRIENDLY SHORES

Is it true some skippers never drag their anchors? In my experience, any skipper who says he never drags is not to be trusted. It happens to all of us, despite our best precautions and techniques. Therefore, if you have a choice in the matter, pick an anchorage with soft or sandy shores as opposed to one with hard granite, limestone or coral. In the first case, should a squall cast you ashore, the yacht will probably be salvageable with less trouble and expense. There is little chance of saving a yacht that drags onto bone-crushing, jagged rocks or coral.

SWINGING ROOM

This will depend on many factors, your rode length and material, underwater hazards, and how much room the other yachts have left you—assuming you weren't smart enough to get into the anchorage early. It also will depend on whether you and the others are anchored to one or two anchors and the manner of anchoring.

Remember, boats anchored first have prior rights. Sometimes this appears quite unfair as is indicated in the following incident.

We were enjoying a wonderful cruise among the Benjamin Islands of the North Channel. We pulled into a bay on the east side of Croker Island for the night. Several yachts were moored along the west and south sides, using one anchor off the stern and a line ashore.

The only other boat in the bay was a large powerboat well out of the way towards the east side and wind-rode away from the shore 150 feet or so.

We anchored carefully, in a spot that seemed well clear of him and settled down for a peaceful evening. As it turned out, although the water was only about 12' deep he had out about 200' of nylon rode. As the fluky, twilight breeze came down over the hills, he swept the east side of the harbor clean. He could have been at least as safe using 40' of chain, and in the process left room for several other boats. We, in turn, should have queried how much rode he had out before we anchored. As it was, we were obliged to move and anchor out in a much less protected area.

EASE OF ESCAPE

Always plan ahead for contingencies. Hopefully, your nights will be peaceful. But what if a storm comes up, and the other boats start dragging? Sometimes it is safer just to get out of there and seek a less crowded spot or even spend the rest of the night in a less desirable spot, perhaps at sea.

Consider escape routes before an emergency strikes. Take bearings and plot courses on your sketch chart before dark. Watch where and how other skippers anchor. It may be blowing and raining with little or no visibility when it comes time to act.

117

INSECTS AND OTHER NUISANCES

In general, the further you are from shore, the less chance of being bothered by mosquitos, sand flies, no-nos or whatever. Sometimes you must learn to live with the little demons in order to have an otherwise secure anchorage for the night.

There are other nuisances to the senses. Avoid sewer outfalls, fish-packing plants and other malodorous situations. Mud creeks and other marshy areas not only smell bad at low tide, but often harbor hordes of nasty insects. While gnats and mosquitos are little more than nuisances, deer flies or greenhead flies leave horrendous wounds that swell up and infect easily. In the tropics, numerous insect bites can cause dangerous infections, especially in children.

I'll not forget the first (and last) time we visited Reedville in Cockrell Creek in the Chesapeake. It was dusk and we thoughtlessly anchored near the fish factories, not knowing what they were. In Reedville they say "it smells like money." But money never smelled so bad to us and we beat a hasty retreat to a less protected spot just inside the mouth of the creek. Better to have the swell disturbing us than the stench of a fish-rendering process.

OTHER ATTRACTIONS AND DISTRACTIONS

You must always take care to anchor out of any channel. Merely hoisting an anchor light is not enough. Be well out of the channel for your own safety. Also, make sure you don't anchor in the way of seaplanes. They don't have the same choices you have.

You may want to avoid places frequented by speed demons in powerboats. Calm anchorages are great places for water-skiing as well as for spending a peaceful day or night at anchor.

Look carefully on your charts for signs of land-based traffic as well. A railroad, highway or airport with heavy, noisy traffic also will disturb your tranquility.

The gifts of nature such as scenery, beaches, coral to dive on, fish and shellfish to catch—even nudist swimming areas —may rate high on your list of desirable anchorage characteristics.

Or you may want to be near shopping, laundry, restaurants, dance halls, bars or whatever meets your needs of the moment. Even those of us who generally prefer peace and solitude don't mind sharing our favorite anchorages with others of similar preference, providing there is not too much togetherness. So, if you come to a harbor with one or two yachts already anchored peacefully, don't snuggle up too close. They may prefer their privacy.

On the other hand, there rarely is any objection to one rowing by, starting up a friendly conversation, and seeing how it proceeds from there. Some of our best cruising friendships have started just this way.

And there is nothing more enjoyable, on occasion, than a shoreside rendezvous, pot-luck supper and the general socializing of the cruising community.

BASIC ANCHORING PROCEDURE

It's a truth worth repeating. Everytime you enter an anchorage where other boats already are secured, you are the center of attention and the spectators will quickly grade you on the caliber of your seamanship.

It pays to take your time. Sometimes, on entering a strange harbor, I will drop the hook just out of the channel, merely to give a few minutes to look around, to orient myself to the chart and harbor features, and to decide where I want to anchor.

Also, it frequently pays to cruise slowly through an anchorage, checking how other boats are anchored—rope or chain, one anchor or two ahead, or Bahamian moor—and how they are riding, wind rode or tide rode.

Ask the other skippers about prevailing wind, about the tide conditions and bottom holding. How much rode do they have out? Are there any hazards you might not have noticed?

Take note of the quality of their rode. You are far safer anchored near yachts using chain than near that fellow who heaved out his anchor attached to a length of light twine.

If the other yachts are moored to two anchors off the bow, or using the Bahamian moor, or any other form of two-anchor mooring, you must take this factor into account. These arrangements restrict the swinging area and if you anchor nearby on one rode while others use two, there are quite apt to be expensive and embarrassing noises in the night.

Select your anchor based on the type of bottom. Use a burying anchor if indicated, avoiding the lightweight if there is much weed, and choosing instead a plow or Bruce. Decide in advance if you expect to need your heaviest bower or sheet anchor. Do you expect severe wind or wave conditions while at anchor? If so, set the best you have at the outset. If in any doubt about the bottom, I prefer a hooking anchor, such as my fisherman, a Northill or a Bruce. My fisherman will catch in almost anything, and at least gives me a chance to pause and think the situation through more thoroughly.

Are you towing a dinghy? Be sure it is snubbed up close to the transom or otherwise secured so the rode cannot possibly get around the propellor while you are backing down. I prefer to tie mine on a short painter either at the midship cleat or to a cleat alongside the cockpit. It's a common problem and a comical one for those spectators, when they see the bow of the dinghy disappear under the stern just before the engine suddenly stops. Some people have an odd sense of humor!

Of course, by now you've got your anchor "at the ready." If you don't have a windlass and a suitable chain or rope locker, you will have gotten your chain out and ranged it out on deck or flaked down the appropriate length of line ready to run.

You've decided whether or not to rig an anchor buoy and trip line. You've checked that all shackles are tight and properly wired.

You've instructed your crew as to your plans and decided who is to do what. Both helmsman and foredeck crew have familiarized themselves with the hand signals you will use.

You know the spot, the depth, the bottom, where the anchor will bury, and you know where the yacht will lie when all is accomplished.

Although the tactic may startle another skipper, it is not necessarily bad practice to drop your anchor just off his stern. When you set it and fall back on your rode, you will be far away from him.

Proceed slowly to the spot where the anchor is to be lowered. Bring the yacht dead in the water, bow to wind or tide, and as you start to fall back, lower the anchor slowly and steadily to the bottom.

As the yacht falls back, either by wind, current, or by engine in reverse, slowly pay out the rode until you have a scope ratio of 3:1 for chain, 5:1 for rope. *Never let the rode fall in a pile on top of the anchor.*

At this point, as the yacht moves astern, snub the line to set the anchor. It may drag momentarily until the fluke catches and it starts to dig in.

Snubbing too hard at this stage may cause it to snatch out rather than to bite into the bottom. When you have fallen back a bit more, put the engine full in reverse for a few moments and watch the rode. If it remains taut, your anchor probably has dug in securely. If it tightens, then becomes loose and keeps up this jerky motion, it undoubtedly is not secure, but if conditions permit you to continue backing down, the anchor may still dig in securely.

If possible, dive on the anchor to check how well it is

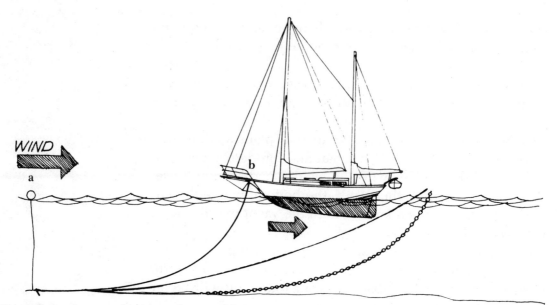

Drop the anchor at point (a), *perhaps with buoy and trip line attached, and pay out rode slowly as you fall back. At* (b), *with a scope ratio of 3:1, snub the rode and back down under power to set the anchor. Then continue to fall back to your final, selected position. Scope ratio depends on the type of rode and the weather conditions in the anchorage with 3:1 the minimum for all chain; 5:1 for half chain half nylon; 7:1 for all nylon. Pay out even more in storm conditions.*

buried or, at the very least, go out in your dinghy with a glass-bottomed bucket and sight your anchor. You may find it is merely snagged on a bit of weed or coral. If real strain comes on the rode this could break off and set you dragging.

If in doubt, weigh and try again in the same place unless you are convinced the spot is totally unsuitable. In this case, try someplace else.

It is essential, even in calm weather, that the anchor dig in. I've often noticed when snorkeling around tropical anchorages that very few anchors have more than the point of the fluke bedded in. This is no good if a storm comes up. If you want to sleep soundly, the anchor must be buried thoroughly or hooked securely.

Don't skimp on rode. *Neither chain nor rope ever does you any good in the locker.* Within reason, put out as much rode as you can given the circumstances, including the amount of scope used by others in the anchorage. But don't let their poor anchoring techniques deter you from doing the right thing. On the other hand, don't put out a whole lot of unnecessary rode and hog the entire anchorage.

For chain: 3:1 is the minimum.
          5:1 is better.
          7:1 or 10:1 for storms, even more for hurricanes.
For rope: 7:1 is the minimum.
          10:1 or greater for storms.

And don't forget to include some shock absorber in the rode.

Remember, the scope ratio is the ratio of the length of rode in use to the sum of 1) depth of water over the anchor at high tide, plus 2) the height to the bow roller or other point of attachment to the yacht. The depth where the yacht comes to rest may be something entirely different.

What is the scope ratio of (a) *and* (b)*?* (a) *is in 10′ of water with a scope ratio of 60/45 or 1.33.* (b) *is in 40′ of water with a scope ratio of 60/15 or 4. Yet* (a) *is more safely anchored with breeze off the land.* (b) *would have to drag only a few feet for the anchor to pull out. Neither is safe if the wind should shift.*

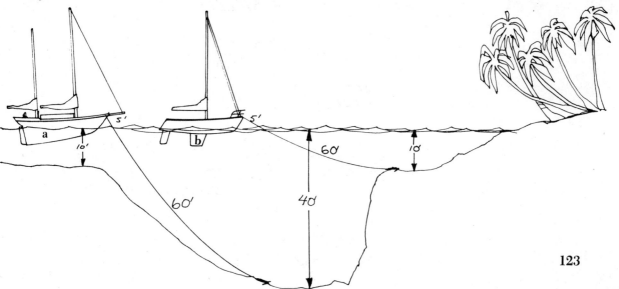

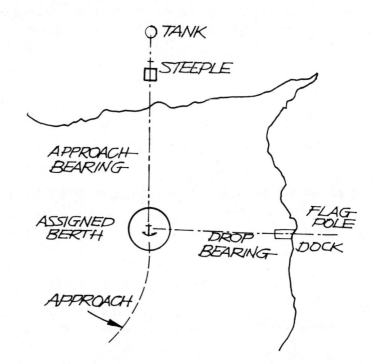

Once anchored, take bearings of objects on shore and of nearby boats. Whenever possible use a range and select lighted objects for bearings so you can identify them at night. You need only two good bearings provided they are approximately 90° apart.

Now take bearings on the shore. Ranges are even better if it is possible to get them. Note your scope ratio, make a sketch of the harbor and other yachts if necessary so you can plan your escape route. When all this is done, rig the awning and relax with a cool drink. It is your turn to be spectator and critic as other boats come to anchor, and to mentally grade their capabilities.

The boat should not be left immediately unless you set an anchor watch. It may be necessary to rig chafing gear or to hang an anchor light in the rigging.

Remember too, that even though you have a crew to do all the work of anchoring while you stay at the wheel and give the orders, it is the skipper's responsibility to ensure that everything is done properly and checked thoroughly.

If the anchorage is beset by swells causing the yacht to roll uncomfortably, a bridle might reduce the movement. Turn the yacht so that the waves hit directly on the bow, if possible.

ETHICS AND RESPONSIBILITIES

Anchoring properly, with consideration for one's neighbors, is simple common sense and good manners—as well as good seamanship.

We talk about consideration for others in many places through this book. Laws may well vary from one country to another. Generally, the boat that anchors first has prior rights and all others are expected to give her swinging room and respect her privacy and security. While you may well expect this treatment at home, the rules may be different somewhere else. Avoid any altercation, especially in another country. It isn't worth the hassle, legal and otherwise.

Should you pick up a permanent mooring without permission, or anchor near an unoccupied mooring so as to interfere with its use, you may be asked to move when the owner returns. Similarly with a buoyed anchor.

125

Avoid dropping your anchor ahead of another yacht, then falling back until your stern is quite close to his bow. You may be perfectly safe but you can expect him to worry about your yacht dragging. Not only have you added to his stress, but you have invaded his privacy and cut his options. How is he going to weigh anchor when you are lying over his rode?

This happened to me one time in the inner hurricane hole on Stocking Island in the Exumas. We were anchored peacefully and relaxing when a beautiful, spit-and-polish power yacht came in and anchored ahead, then backed down until his transom was only 6 feet or so off to one side of my bow pulpit. I suggested to one of the men in the aft cockpit, where a group were enjoying their drinks, that this type of anchoring was creating a hazard. He replied that the captain was a professional and knew what he was doing. That certainly wasn't obvious. What can one do in such cases?

I made a point of standing on my foredeck, sharpening the end of my boathook with a file. In a few moments they moved, but only pulled ahead a few feet. It takes all types!

What are the responsibilities when the anchorage is hit by a gale and boats start to drag? By age-old customs of the

(a) *anchored first. You may drop your anchor off his stern and fall back out of his way, as at* (c). ***Do not anchor ahead, otherwise as you fall back you will be very near him, as in*** (b).

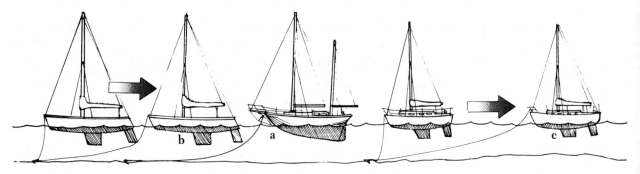

brotherhood of the sea, every sailor will try to help another in distress as long as he is not putting his own vessel and crew in jeopardy. The first responsibility is to life and limb. Property comes later, even though usually the two issues go hand in hand. When yachts start to drag, each skipper will ensure, so far as he is able, that his own boat is safe and secure, then do what he can to help the others.

LIGHTS, SHAPES AND SOUND SIGNALS

Earlier we discussed the equipment for anchor lights and shapes. Unfortunately, these are not seen often enough.

Remember, you are required by law to show these lights or shapes except in areas designated as anchorages by the Coast Guard or other authority.

When anchored in reduced visibility you are expected to sound a bell for about five seconds every minute.

You may get away without using proper signals, in fact many skippers do break this law frequently. Too often, the importance of the light or sphere is only determined at the inquest, after the accident.

ANCHOR WATCH

Frequently it is desirable to have someone assigned to anchor watch.

The minimum responsibility is to check for drag, check the anchor light, check for chafe, check that the yacht does not swing near a hazard or too near other yachts—and also that the latter don't swing too close to you.

The watchkeeper must alert the skipper if anything requires attention beyond his own ability to cope. Often the skipper, who always has the ultimate responsibility on his or her shoulders, retains anchor watch duty. In the first half hour or so after anchoring he will check frequently, almost constantly. In a gale or worse, the anchor watch is constant, though mostly from shelter, with excursions forward as needed.

When the skipper and party go ashore and leave someone on board, that crew member is usually left for several purposes. He or she may have some specific chore to do that is best done on an empty boat, such as tearing apart and rebuilding the head. He also will be charged with boat watch —repelling unwanted boarders, etc. Anchor watch is not the least of duties and so the crew member must be capable of dealing with any and all problems associated with the ground tackle. If necessary, he may have to take out a second anchor, or weigh anchor and move to another spot. Finally, he or she may be required to weigh, to set sail and leave harbor for the open sea.

The responsibility assigned must be clarified in advance between skipper and the crewmember assigned the watch.

ANCHOR ALARMS

Sometimes an anchor watch is either impossible or does not seem necessary. It would be nice to have some ingenious electronic device that would waken us when the yacht drags.

There are many products on the market that do this. Even though we are surrounded by high technology, let's look at a simple, low-tech system. Your leadline and a frying pan (surely you have both on board) comprise the only ingredients of the system.

Lower the lead to the bottom with enough slack to accommodate the normal back and forth sheering.

Attach the bitter end of the lead line to a frying pan sitting on the cabin top (or some other precarious position).

When the leadline tightens, the frying pan falls off onto the deck with a clatter. Be sure to have another cord attached so you don't lose the whole works over the side.

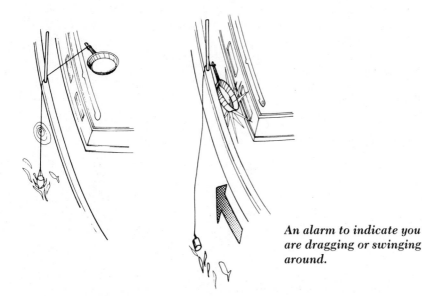

An alarm to indicate you are dragging or swinging around.

Another simple alarm will warn you if the wind makes up in the night.

It consists of ranging out perhaps 12 to 20′ of rode, either rope or chain, on the deck and securing the rode to a deck fitting with a short piece of light line, so that the line takes the strain.

As the wind increases, the line breaks and the rode lying on deck starts to run out. With chain, anyone sleeping below is bound to wake up. With rope, while you may hear nothing, the jolt as the yacht snubs at the end of the line usually will waken the crew.

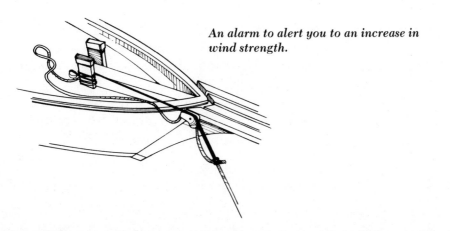

An alarm to alert you to an increase in wind strength.

129

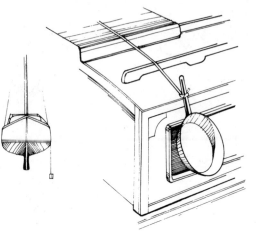

A "low-tide" alarm.

Although not as reliable an indication of dragging, and one you shouldn't count on, there is frequently a distinct change in motion when the yacht is dragging. If dragging free, the yacht often will turn sideways to the wind and swell.

There is a simple alarm for low tide that you may want to use some night. Lower a weight over the side so it is slightly below the keel. Attach the end of the line to something like your old reliable frying pan, which is hanging in the hatchway. When the weight touches bottom, the tension on the line is reduced and the frying pan falls to the deck, awakening the crew.

OTHER ANCHOR-SETTING METHODS

The method described previously is only one way to set the anchor. It is satisfactory for both powerboats and sailboats providing the wind or current and/or engine is strong enough to bury the anchor when backing down.

Other methods are just as satisfactory. If the wind or tide will cooperate, or when you are shorthanded, try this technique.

Decide where you want to set the anchor. Check depth and bottom, hazards and swinging room as described previously. Proceed upwind or upcurrent of that spot. Turn around and proceed back over the spot slowly at one or two knots—under sail, engine or perhaps just current-power.

Lower the anchor at the selected spot, pay out the rode as previously, then snub briefly. This will usually set the anchor unless you are moving too fast. In this case, the anchor may drag rather than set. Under extreme conditions, (going much too fast) snubbing could damage deck fittings. Hence, keep that speed down.

At once, lower sail or shut off the engine and the boat will

Coming to anchor downwind in crowded quarters: lower the anchor, pay line out slowly and steadily, snub it to set the anchor and lower sails as the yacht swings to wind or tide.

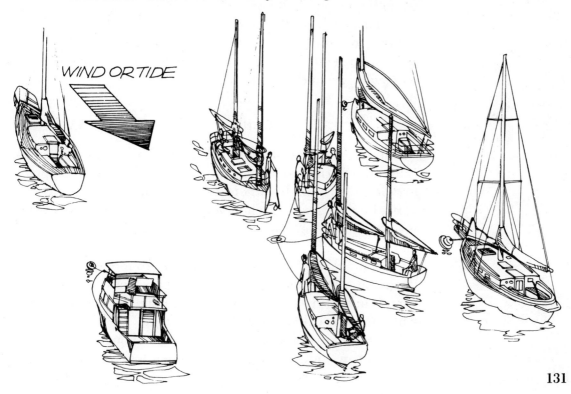

WIND OR TIDE

quickly turn end-for-end and you can then veer all the rode you wish and drift back down.

This procedure is very effective with fishermen, plow or Bruce anchors snubbing at 3:1 scope. A lightweight with chain rode will probably need 5:1 scope, perhaps 7:1, if rope.

Providing you are going at a suitable speed, one to two knots, there is nothing in your way, it doesn't really matter whether you are running downwind, reaching, beating, or under power. The pull caused by the moving yacht usually will set the anchor.

However, keep in mind the way the yacht will lie after you have come to rest. It is important to have the pull directly on the anchor. Only the plow is designed to withstand a pulling force from the side. Other anchors may break out or be damaged, though they generally will turn in line if there is enough tension on the rode.

On a small boat it is practical to set the anchor under way by lowering it over the stern. Then, after coming to rest, the rode can be taken around to the stem, at which time the yacht will swing around to lie facing the anchor.

FLYING, RUNNING OR BAHAMIAN MOOR

Anchoring to two anchors while under way, sometimes called the flying moor or running moor (if it doesn't happen to work, it's called by other, less complimentary names) is a very effective method when you want to restrict your swinging room, or when you must anchor in a place where wind and currents reverse direction frequently. This could be in a narrow creek that dries out at low tide except for a narrow, deep-water channel, or in a tidal stream or passage between coral, such as is frequently found in the Bahamas. There, naturally, it is called the Bahamian moor.

Whether moving under sail or power is immaterial, providing wind and tide are favorable. There are several ways to do it.

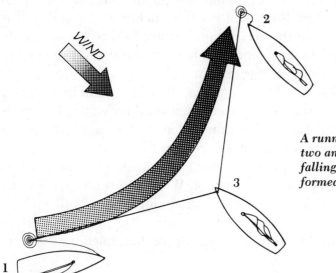

A running moor consists of laying two anchors "on the run" and falling back into the angle formed between the two rodes.

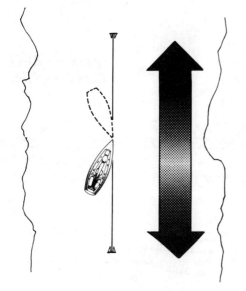

The Bahamian moor: Two anchors used in a narrow channel to restrict swinging as the tide or current changes.

Drop the first anchor on the run, paying out twice as much rode as needed. Snub and set this anchor at the end of this rode, then drop the second underfoot. Pull in the first rode until you are halfway between the two. Now pull tight on the second rode and set that anchor.

Both rodes should come to the stem. They can be fastened together and the junction lowered into the water. If rope is used, a weight at the junction will keep the lines low enough so they won't foul the keel or rudder.

Never use a stern anchor and a bow anchor together unless a constant anchor watch is kept. Wind and waves hitting the yacht abeam can exert tremendous forces and pull out the anchors.

The second method is to lower the first anchor at the up-

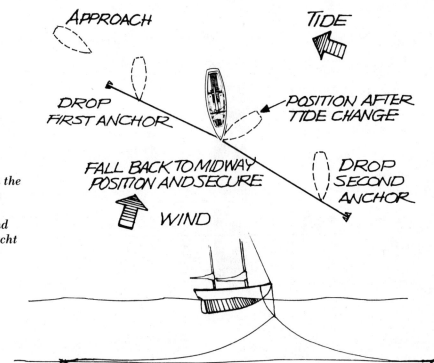

Drop the first anchor on the run, pay out rode as you proceed to the second position. Drop the second anchor and pull your yacht back to the midway position setting both anchors as you do.

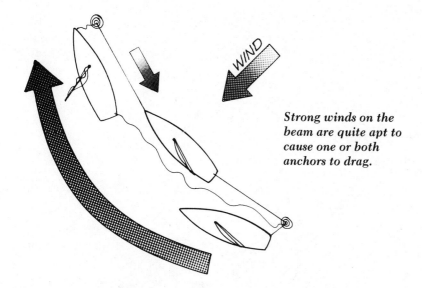

Strong winds on the beam are quite apt to cause one or both anchors to drag.

wind or upcurrent point, fall back on twice the needed rode, setting it as you go. Then lower the second anchor. Now pull in on the first rode until the yacht is halfway between the two. Set the second anchor and secure both lines at the bow as before.

If there is much tidal range, it may be necessary to pay out more rode at high tide and reduce the rode again as the tide falls in order to reduce your swinging room.

Similar procedure may be used to place two anchors when broadreaching.

Select the two spots, have everything ready on deck and lower each anchor as you pass over the selected spots, paying out plenty of rode. Get all sail off quickly and let the wind carry the yacht back to the apex of the "V," at which point you must put enough force on the individual rodes to set and bury the anchors.

I am personally opposed to anchoring with chain ranged out on deck or with rope flaked down on deck, because of the

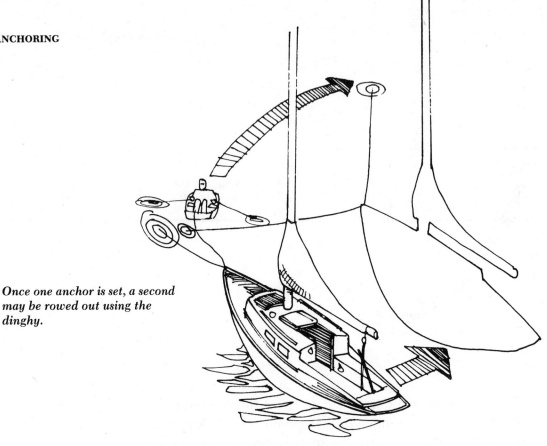

Once one anchor is set, a second may be rowed out using the dinghy.

inherent danger to crew, although sometimes it is necessary to anchor on the run.

Also, when using two anchors, I consider it particularly important to buoy them both.

Again, it pays in worry-free sleep, to sight the anchors before considering the anchoring procedure complete.

One final method for setting a Bahamian moor is to set one in the normal fashion, and row out the second in the dinghy. We will describe this method in more detail later.

SINGLEHANDED ANCHORING

There are two common methods of dropping an anchor with no one up forward.

Bring a rope rode, out from the bow, putting it through a

136

chock or over the bow roller, back to the stern outside all shrouds and stanchions. Secure the rode to an anchor at the stern or in the cockpit. The rode can be secured to a stern cleat if you wish, or secured only at the bow. In either case there should be enough line between cleat and anchor to give a 5:1 scope ratio with most anchors, 7:1 with a lightweight.

Now proceed to the selected spot. The anchor is close at hand and can be dropped over the side or off the stern when you reach that spot, preferably going slowly downwind or current.

For this procedure, when no one is on the foredeck, it is quite practical to flake out the line ahead of time. In fact, it is very important that the operation be thoroughly prepared in advance. Should a tangle materialize in the line up forward

Anchoring singlehanded with rope or chain rode.

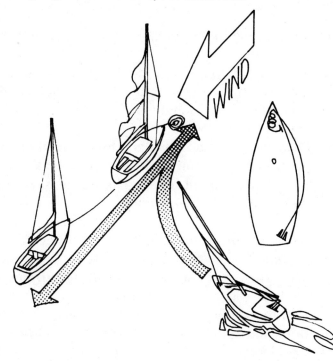

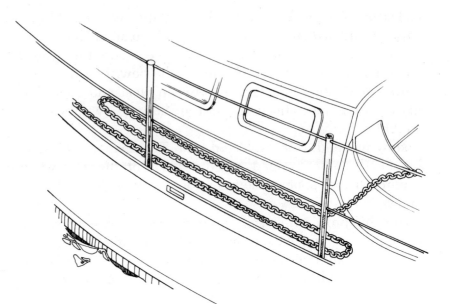

Chain ranged out on deck.

while you are steering in the cockpit, everything can go haywire.

We all have our preferred methods. My first choice, when shorthanded, is to rig a toggle hitch to the chain, which quickly can be tripped by a light line brought back to the cockpit.

I lower the anchor over the roller and let it hang there with the chain either ranged out on deck or else the brake off the chain gypsy so it can run out freely. The toggle hitch holds the chain from running until I am ready.

On passing the selected spot, I pull the toggle, the chain is released, the anchor drops to the bottom and I have time to walk forward to attend to the rest of the procedure—snubbing to set the anchor when enough chain is run out and making the rode fast when the anchor is set.

Of course, if the chain is ranged out, say three times the depth, it can be secured and the anchor will be set before I ever have to go forward.

Dale Nouse, *Cruising World* magazine's editor-at-large, has described to me an even simpler system, particularly suited to a rope rode.

The anchor is arranged "at the ready," hanging from the bow roller or chock. A bight of the rode is pulled back to the cockpit, inside the shrouds, where it is cleated in place.

When you arrive at the selected spot, merely uncleat the rode and pay it out while you are going astern slowly, snubbing when you have adequate rode out. (Be sure the rode cannot snag on any deck fitting.)

At your leisure, go forward and cleat the rode properly, making all ready for weighing.

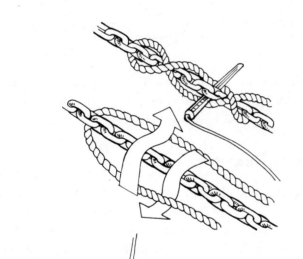

A simple toggle arrangement for chain and another for rope. Pulling out the toggle releases the rode to permit lowering the anchor from the bow without your leaving the cockpit.

TOGGLE

139

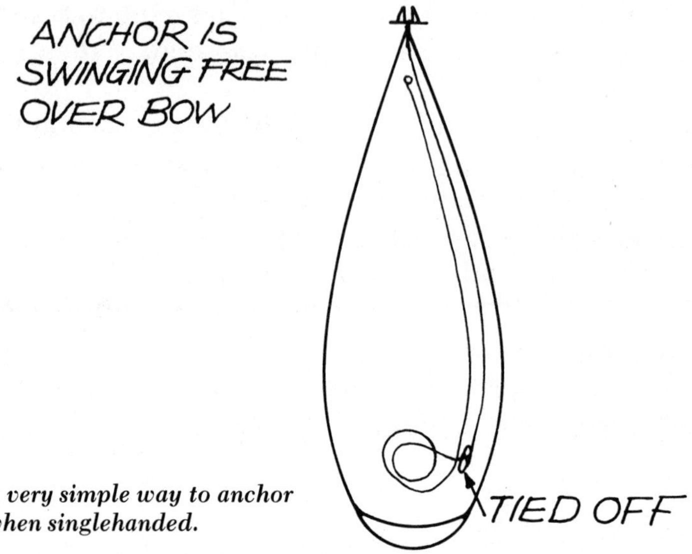

ANCHOR IS
SWINGING FREE
OVER BOW

A very simple way to anchor
when singlehanded.

TIED OFF

The single-hander can easily set two anchors without ever leaving the cockpit using the procedures just described.

EMERGENCY BRAKES

Having an anchor at the stern ready to let go at a moment's notice is a wise precaution whenever you are maneuvering in close quarters. It can prove a very important source of security if a bridgetender doesn't open the bridge as promptly as you might wish, or if the crew on the foredeck gets into difficulties lowering the main anchor and you are heading downwind too fast with someone else's yacht not far ahead.

If you are cruising at a good clip, the anchor may not set or it might pull the stern cleat out if you are not careful. Sheets, of course, should be eased and the engine, if on, put in idle. The trick is to snub the rode gently and slow the boat down before really letting the anchor pull you to an abrupt stop. Watch your hands on that line. It can be dangerous, but less so than a collision with a bridge.

Des Sleightholme tells of a story sent in to him as editor of *Yachting Monthly* recently. A Thames lockkeeper was watching the boats entering a crowded lock and in particular a motor cruiser tearing in far too fast. "Go astern, go astern!" yelled the lockkeeper urgently. The helmsman of the cruiser was not a man to ignore expert advice, however strange it might sound to him. Leaving the wheel he quickly nipped aft and sat down by his wife in the stern. A stern anchor probably wouldn't have been much help anyway.

I roam the commercial harbors every chance I get. Once I was watching a huge laker coming alongside the harbor wall at Goderich to take on a load of salt. I was surprised to see the skipper drop his big port bower anchor and drag it along the channel bottom solely to slow the boat down.

Some time later, I had an opportunity to go aboard a different ship and chat with the master while he was taking on a load of salt. I inquired about the anchor dragging incident and he told me this story.

Another master, let's call him Captain Ted, was a very good, very conscientious but somewhat nervous skipper. His nervous tension seemed to peak whenever he had to bring his heavy ship into harbor.

One time, it seemed to Captain Ted that he was coming in much too fast, a situation most of us have experienced in our own much smaller boats. He felt the adrenaline flow.

"Drop the stern anchor," he called out excitedly. A moment later, "Drop the port anchor."

The ship was slowing but the dock was approaching too fast. Sweating heavily, he ordered, "Drop the starboard anchor." A short time later the lines were made fast and the vessel secured. The mate came aft.

"A very narrow escape, Captain. We stopped just in time."

The skipper, who was starting to calm down, turned, "Were you nervous we were going to hit the dock?" challenged the skipper, who now felt a bit defensive.

"No," replied the mate. "I was worried you'd call for another anchor, when we had no more to drop."

141

WHY SET TWO ANCHORS?

Using two anchors and two rodes is a very common technique, far too common to my way of thinking. I admit there are many times when two anchors are essential—the Bahamian moor, for example. Before you set two anchors, think it through thoroughly. What do you expect to accomplish? Remember, one anchor, properly selected and set, with proper rode, is far better than two that are not being used correctly.

Among the ways two or more anchors are sometimes used to advantage, are:

1. Two off the bow at various angles to increased holding power and to decrease swinging.
2. A second set off to one side or the other to limit the swing. Sometimes called the "hammerlock."
3. One out forward, the second one set aft 180° apart with both rodes brought to the stem. This is the popular Bahamian moor, used to limit swing and to keep a boat in place in wildly shifting currents and wind.
4. Two anchors in tandem used to increase holding power.
5. Two, three, even four anchors, all brought to the stem, used as a hurricane mooring.

You frequently will see boats secured with two anchors off the bow regardless of current or weather. The skippers seem to believe that if one anchor is good, two must be better.

In general, this is quite unnecessary, and most of the time serves very little purpose. Granted, it does reduce the swinging area somewhat and it does provide a backup in case one anchor fails or a rode parts. It is far better to be sure that one anchor system is sound and properly set. Generally, two anchors do not share the strain except under very limited conditions of swing. Ninety percent of the time the entire strain is on one anchor or the other.

The holding power of two anchors set at a 90° angle varies

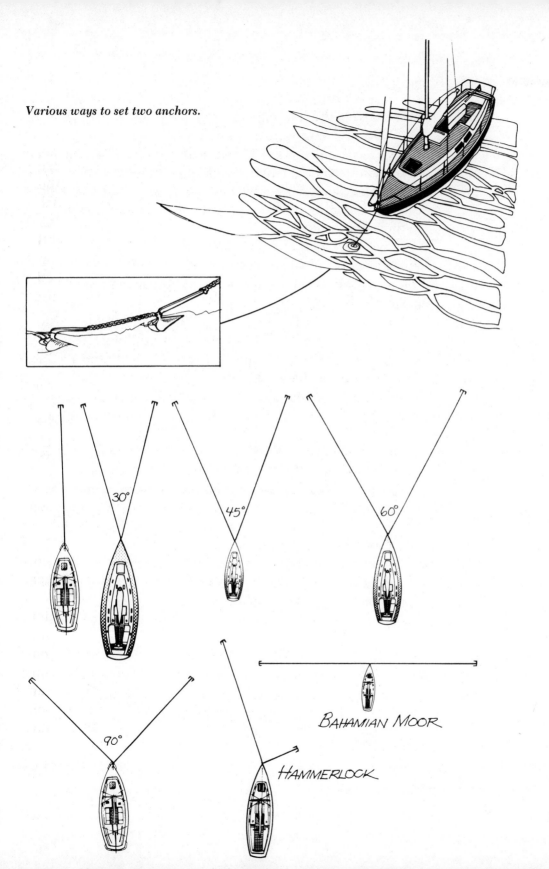

Various ways to set two anchors.

30°

45°

60°

90°

BAHAMIAN MOOR

HAMMERLOCK

143

from 100% of the holding power of one to 140% of the power, not 200%, as some appear to think.

Two dead ahead is 200%, two at 180° only 100%. The need to buoy the anchors is increased when more than one is set.

The two rodes can get twisted together and this can be the cause of one or both being pulled out, causing the pair to fail in their purpose.

However, when it is necessary to limit the swing of the yacht because of some hazard off to one side, then there is sound reason to set a second anchor, off at right angles, opposite the hazard.

If there is no wind or current forcing the boat to one side, this second anchor can be set abeam or off the stern. This is a common practice in streams to keep the yacht from a hazard such as shore or shallows.

Should the current change as in a tidal stream, or should a strong wind come up abeam, this is not a satisfactory solution.

The wind hitting the topsides broadside will exert a very strong force indeed and might pull out the anchors.

The use of two anchors in tandem is an excellent way to reduce the danger of dragging. This system gives the full holding power of two anchors. It is a very effective and satisfactory arrangement in very heavy weather.

If the bottom appears suitable, the anchors may be the same, lightweights, fishermen or whatever. My preference is to combine a fisherman at the end of the rode with a plow or lightweight 20 to 30′ up the rode. I join the two with chain

Two anchors properly set in tandem have tremendous holding power.

and would have great reservations about using nylon for two reasons: You don't want any stretch between the two anchors and nylon might chafe on something on the bottom.

The preferred arrangement is to use a separate length of chain between the two anchors, attached to the crown of the one nearest the yacht. Alternatively, if you attach the nearer anchor to a point 20 to 30′ up the rode, lash its crown to the rode.

MOORING WITH ANCHORS

Should you want to set a mooring and plan on leaving the yacht unoccupied for a prolonged time, you must take extra precautions. Otherwise, you will have good reason to worry constantly while away.

It is best to set three anchors, each on chain, 120° apart. Bring the chains together near the center of the triangle and attach a swivel at this point being certain to wire each shackle pin. Then run another, (preferably heavier) chain from the yacht to the swivel. Use some nylon snubbers between mooring chain and the boat.

You are now protected as well as possible from all directions of wind. To be certain someone doesn't anchor nearby and inadvertently hook and raise one of your rodes, buoy each anchor.

Setting out three anchors in this manner almost certainly requires a second boat but it is not too difficult to do with your dinghy. Read the next section on setting out a second anchor with the dinghy.

Well-known Lin and Larry Pardey left their beloved *Seraffyn* in the Sea of Cortez some years ago to make a yacht delivery. This is how they set a mooring, as described in "Cruising in *Seraffyn*" (Seven Seas Press, 1976).

> We'd be away for several weeks, and we wanted to be certain our boat would be secure. To begin with, we set our 22-

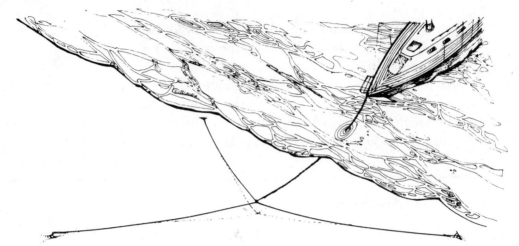

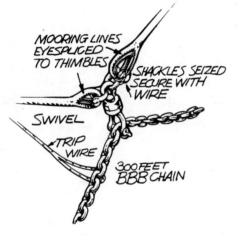

MOORING LINES
EYESPLICED
TO THIMBLES

SHACKLES SEIZED
SECURE WITH
WIRE

SWIVEL

TRIP
WIRE

300 FEET
BBB CHAIN

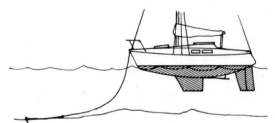

AFTER ANCHORING NORMALLY
ATTACH SWIVEL WITH LONG MOORING-
LINE TO CENTER OF ANCHOR CHAIN.

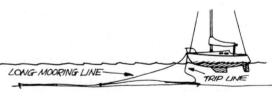

LONG MOORING LINE

TRIP LINE

DRIFT BACK WITH WIND OR CURRENT
PAYING OUT LONG MOORING LINE AND
REMAINDER OF CHAIN SET. SECOND
ANCHOR ON CHAIN WITH TRIPLINE.

SWIVEL

LOWER SWIVEL INTO WATER TO BELOW
DEPTH OF KEEL AND SECURE BOTH MOOR-
ING LINES WITH WELL ATTACHED CHAFING GEAR.

146

pound Danforth anchor and lowered half of our 300 feet of chain. At the mid-point we shackled on a swivel to which we led a long line. Then we drifted downwind, paying out the rest of the chain until we reached the bitter end. Here we attached our 33-pound kedge and dropped it overboard with a long trip line. Then we hauled the boat back to the swivel, attached two ⅝″ nylon lines to it with shackles, and secured each shackle with a wire seizing. We lowered the swivel into the water until it was below our keel and cleated the two ⅝″ lines on deck with good chafing gear on them.

USING A DINGHY TO SET AN ANCHOR

We've discussed setting one anchor or two or three. Quite often these can be set by the mother yacht. Sometimes—especially when setting three anchors—this is not practical.

When you have to set more than one anchor, often it is because danger threatens—a storm is brewing or maybe you're aground. These techniques could save your yacht and your lives, so read carefully.

I am not going to get into the controversy of whether a hard, rowing dinghy is better than an inflatable. I always select a good, hard dinghy. If you can row out your inflatable —carrying a 40 lb. anchor, plus some chain and a long rode —into a strong wind and heavy seas, I'll eat a can of your spinach!

For the remainder of this discussion, I will assume you have a dinghy that you can handle under such circumstances.

It is impractical, generally, to set an all-chain rode in a dinghy. Usually it is all rope, or at least nearly so. Special technique is necessary whenever considerable chain is used. It can be done with a reasonable quantity of chain, providing you and the dinghy can handle it.

First, work out hand signals with someone in the yacht who will direct you. It is impossible to hear shouted signals in storm conditions.

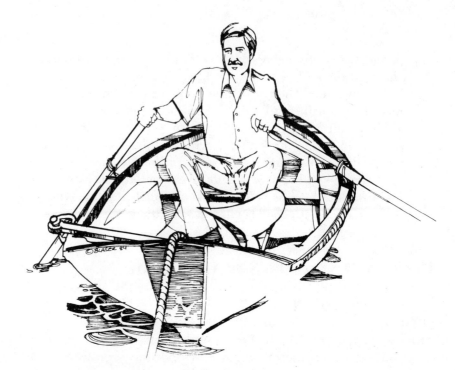

Carrying out an anchor in the dinghy is a skill every cruising man should know. It must be possible to drop the anchor without changing the balance of the dinghy.

Do not pay out the line from the yacht. Put it all into the dinghy. Do this carefully and properly, as follows:

Suspend the anchor over the dinghy transom with light line tied back to your thwart, or alternatively, hook it over the transom where you can easily reach it without having to move around in the dinghy. Carry a sharp knife in a sheath at your belt or lay it on the thwart beside you. Find an arrangement so that the anchor will not accidentally hook up when you want to drop it. I've had trouble with my fisherman that way. It's an awkward thing to handle at any time and I found the only solution was to suspend it over the transom.

Flake down the line on the floor of the dinghy so that it will run easily. The last thing you want is a tangle of rode under these conditions. It will help if the rode runs out over one spot on the transom where you can brake the run with your foot, while continuing to row.

Now, secure the bitter end of the rode to a cleat or bitt at the bow, after running it through a chock. Push off and row hard toward your target. It will be difficult work. Take short, strong strokes and feather the oars on the back stroke. Feathering makes a very noticeable difference. Be prepared for an exhausting job in storm conditions.

As you row away from the yacht, usually directly into the wind and current, the rode will pay out from the dinghy behind you until you come to the end. Never row across the wind or current if it can be avoided.

Row as hard as you can and with a sudden burst of power you can even pay out a few feet of chain, providing you don't let up on your efforts.

Stretch the line to its maximum and instantly grab the knife and cut the line holding the anchor to the transom.

Now, back to the yacht and haul in the rode to set the anchor.

There is a simple trick to make this setting of the second anchor easier, for you will lose a lot of the rode in setting and burying the anchor. Secure about 50' of light line between the yacht and the bitter end of the rode. Sure, you have to row 50' further, but the result is far more satisfactory. By the time you have hauled in the light line, the anchor usually is thoroughly set and you now have the bitter end of the rode on board and secured. Make sure the lighter line is capable of absorbing the strain of snubbing.

Now here is a technique that will let you handle an even heavier anchor, plus a fair length of chain, with little difficulty even in heavy seas. It does take some planning, however, and a bit more time. It is a very effective ploy, easy to carry out.

Take a light anchor into the dinghy, a long length of light line and an anchor buoy. If you have sufficient light line, you don't need the buoy. We are going to set the light anchor at a selected spot, far upwind, then haul the dinghy and heavy anchor out to it using the light line.

If you haven't enough light line to reach from the selected spot to the yacht, this is where the buoy comes in. The wind will blow it towards the yacht. When you row out with the heavy anchor and rode, you pick up the buoy and pull yourself the rest of the way on the light line.

If it reaches all the way, you haul the dinghy out as far as you want, drop the heavy anchor, pick up the light anchor and row back.

Note that the light line must be flaked in the dinghy differently if you are going to pay it out while attached to the yacht than if you are going to drop the anchor at the selected spot, then pay out the line with the buoy at the end.

Once you have dropped the heavy anchor, there is no need to leave the light one in place. Break it out, take it into the dinghy and back to the yacht.

As I indicated, this is more time-consuming and only is needed in the worst of circumstances, but it shows what can be done with a little imagination.

Des Sleightholme, editor of *Yachting Monthly* offered another technique in the December, 1978 issue. I haven't tried it but it sounds quite practical.

Put your heavy kedge into the dinghy with no rode attached. Tow a long light line astern from the dinghy feeding it out from yacht to dinghy as you row upwind as far as you can.

Anchor the dinghy with a light anchor.

Haul out the rode, which your crew has attached to the aforementioned light line. Having some chain in the rode will help but it should be brought out in the dinghy.

Attach the rode to the anchor and lower it over the stern of the dinghy.

Now, raise the light anchor and row back while your crew hauls in the rode, sets the kedge anchor and buries it.

These methods are not simple but they do work and are good to try first when conditions are benign. Then you will know how to use them when conditions get wild.

SWIMMING OUT AN ANCHOR

The same technique applies to swimming the anchor out. It may sound difficult, but it's not impossible. I'll let Lin and Larry Pardey tell you how they did it, in the Gulf of Suez, as written in *Cruising World* in January, 1984.

We dove over and swam along our anchor chain. To the amazement of both of us, our anchor hadn't moved at all. But the three-foot-high coral head that had been just behind our anchor now lay split and toppled, torn from its roots by our chain. That explained the horrendous noise we'd heard the night before.

"I need a good night's sleep," Larry said when he came up for air. "Let's set another anchor. Besides, I want to try something new." So rather than get the dinghy overboard, he took a fender and tied it to our 12-pound Danforth anchor. He then swam just below the chop, his snorkel tracing a straight and accurate course to windward as he pulled our 200-foot warping line. I payed the line out from the foredeck and secured it after he dove down and set the small anchor. Then he tied the fender around his waist and pulled himself back along the new anchor line. We tied three fenders to our 35-pound fisherman with its 30 feet of chain and 300-foot long ⅝-inch nylon rode. I payed the rode out as he pulled himself and the floating anchor along the first line. When he untied the fenders the anchor fell into position 150 feet ahead of *Seraffyn*. Larry pulled up the 12-pounder and I reeled him back in.

"That worked easily," he said when he was back on board. "I think I could have done that last night if I'd thought of it." I agreed that it would have been worth a try since he'd never once been detached from the boat during the whole maneuver and he hadn't had to fight the windage of the dinghy. It probably would have worked.

A few hours later I was glad we had two anchors out. The wind rose until it was blowing at least as fiercely as it had been the night before. But with no uninvited Egyptian soldiers, no submachine guns on board and two anchors set, we got a very good night's sleep.

151

DEFENSIVE ANCHORING

All who ever share crowded anchorages have experienced being awakened from a sound sleep by the annoying and expensive noise of two boats bumping together. It happens quite frequently, often when there are no conditions which would cause drag.

I've been tempted, on a squally, wet night to hit the berth fully clothed, oilies and seaboots, ready for action. So far, I've refrained from doing it.

Several have written of being so startled by the noise and the shouting, that they've dashed on deck only to realize, too late, they were stark naked. So far, I've avoided that, too.

Fortunately the crash that so disturbs our sleep is more often a gentle bump, but the effect usually is the same. Sometimes it seems as though the hull, right by your ear, must be stove in a foot.

ESTIMATING SWINGING ROOM

The reason, of course, may be anchors dragging—usually theirs—but sometimes even your own. More often it is due to improperly estimating swinging room.

Swinging room is the area you occupy as your boat swings with wind and tide. It is often called the swinging circle but rarely is circular in shape.

Let's look at a few possibilities:

1. When you are moored with a bow line ashore and one or two anchors set off the stern, your swinging room is really little more than the space occupied by the yacht. Certainly you may move a little to one side or the other, as influenced by wind or tide, but the movement is relatively minor. Remember, though, that the forces here can be strong enough to break out your anchor. This has happened all too frequently in the so-called Mediterranean moor and once one's

yacht anchors yield, the whole row can tumble like domi-
noes. A great deal of damage can result.

2. At the other extreme, look at the case of a 40′ boat trail-
ing a 10′ dinghy on a 20′ painter and anchored in 12′ of water
with a 7:1 scope. (12′ water depth plus 5′ to bow roller.)

The maximum swinging room thus is a circle 2(7 × 17 +
40 + 10 + 20) = 378′ in diameter. It is customary to ignore
the fact that the rode is angled down to the anchor which,
admittedly, reduces the circle by a very small increment.

That is an awfully large chunk out of most anchorages. If
everyone anchored that way, there wouldn't be room for
many boats.

3. If you use a Bahamian moor, and your rodes only have
enough slack to ensure they don't tangle the keel or rudder,
the swinging room is an oval as illustrated.

4. Now, suppose you anchored with two anchors set at 60°
off the bow. Refer to the illustration that shows the swinging
circles you would have occupied on either anchor individ-

The dotted shape shows the swinging area of a yacht anchored with two anchors in the Bahamian moor.

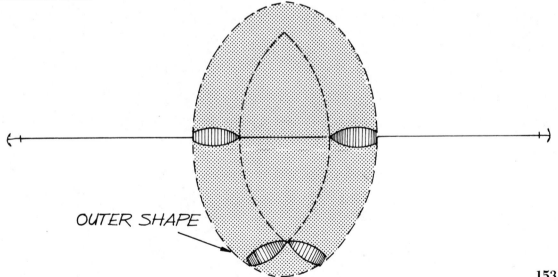

OUTER SHAPE

ually. The shaded portion, the space you could occupy with this arrangement, is about ⅓ what you could have used with either one.

Setting your two anchors 90° apart cuts down the swinging room even more.

5. To complete the picture, we've anchored in a stream and set an anchor off to one side to keep us from blowing ashore. The same applies when you set an anchor merely to limit your swing towards a hazard. The current, or wind keeps you headed in one direction (upstream) and so the swinging area is minimal.

These bumps wouldn't happen, of course, if all of us anchored far enough away from the others, but it just doesn't work that way.

The dotted circle shows the swinging area you would have occupied with only one anchor. The shaded area shows how this space is reduced by setting two anchors 60° apart.

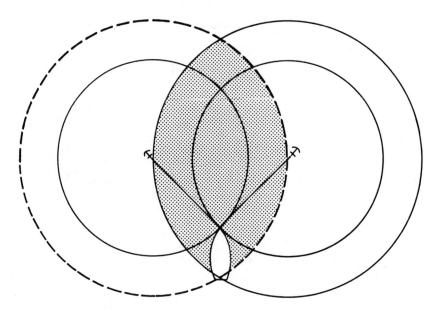

WIND RODE VS. TIDE RODE

Whenever you anchor with other boats in a crowded anchorage, insofar as it can be arranged, ensure that all boats in proximity anchor in the same fashion. Then they can be expected to swing in unison with one another. Well, can't they? Certainly not. That is wishful thinking.

Some may be wind-rode (usually the high-sided powerboats) and will lie bow to wind.

The deep keel boats are quite apt to be tide-rode as the current exerts more pull on their deep undersides, so they face bow to tide.

And what about those that have moderate underwater shape and moderate topside windage? They are apt to be facing any which way.

Also, as the tide changes, or the breeze reverses, boats anchored on long nylon lines are apt to swing much sooner than those that have set out a chain rode that is dragging slowly across the bottom.

The result of all these circumstances? Expensive noises, collisions, confusion, irate skippers and crews, and jangled nerves. That is not what we go cruising for.

SAILING AT ANCHOR

Then there are the yachts that sail at anchor like a spirited horse chomping at the bit: particularly yachts with high windage up forward, the cat-rigged boats and the ultra-lights. They will sheer back and forth with no thought for their neighbors. There is no synchronization to this phenomenon. Your yacht may be sheering to port while your neighbor is going to starboard. The result—frequent collisions. How to reduce the problem?

1. Chain has the advantage over rope as it creates much more friction as it drags across the bottom, also because the scope is shorter.

155

A sentinel dragging on the bottom or a second anchor on its own rode will help limit swing.

2. A sentinel dragging across the bottom just under the bow is a big help, again due to friction on the bottom. Alternately drop a second anchor and veer just enough rode to ensure that the anchor lies on the bottom. As the boat tends to sheer off to one side or the other, the friction of dragging the sentinel or the second anchor will reduce the tendency.

3. An anchor set at the extreme of the sheer to either side will help until the wind shifts.

4. A bridle usually will ensure that your yacht sheers off in one direction only. Tie a suitable line to your anchor rode, outside the bow roller or chock and bring it back to the stern (all outside). If you want the boat to be off on port tack put the bridle on the port side, and vice versa. Secure the line to a stern cleat then slowly let out a few feet of rode. The boat should head off on port tack and stay there. Remember, though, that you have increased the windage and therefore the strain on your rode.

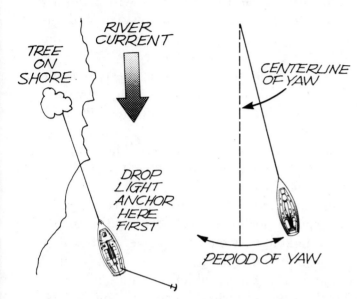 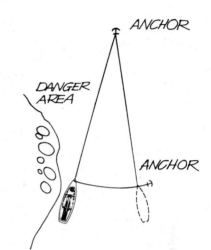

An anchor set at one extreme of the sheer to limit the swing.

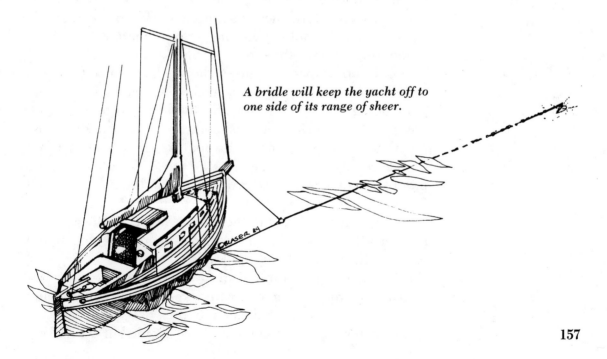

A bridle will keep the yacht off to one side of its range of sheer.

157

5. A mizzen sheeted flat and dead center will generally reduce the tendency to yaw. It must be flat however, and this may necessitate adding and using reef points. Otherwise, the noise of the sail flapping may be a disturbance.

Alternatively, add a small storm jib (or a specially-made "handkerchief" riding sail) attached to the back stay and hardened down forward. It doesn't have to be sheeted amidships.

6. On some boats, anchoring by the stern will help, particularly those boats with a great deal of windage up forward, such as some modern catboats.

Stern anchoring does create problems, however, usually caused by careless powerboaters who expect that the anchor rode is off the bow and cut very close to the stern. They may cut your rode. Try buoying it with a plastic milk jug just where it enters the water. Other problems include rain coming down the hatch, waves entering the cockpit, and similar inconveniences.

If you do try stern anchoring, use a bridle so that the rode comes amidships at the transom, not on a quarter.

Sheering exposes three or four times as much boat surface to wind and waves. It causes the anchor shank to swing widely from side to side. Some anchors will not take this, the plow being the only one specifically designed to cope with this problem. Furthermore, sheering drags the rode across the bottom and increases chafe. So, take all possible precautions to reduce sheer as it can be the cause of many anchoring problems, such as the one Ralph Naranjo described in *Wind Shadow West* (Hearst, 1983). Two yachts were anchored in a rolly bight in Rarotonga in the South Pacific during a severe northerly. As could be expected, one sheered to the east, the other to the west and they collided.

Initial damage was minor until masts and spreaders tangled as they rolled. Rigging parted, spreaders splintered and one mast was literally shaken out of the boat.

All anchorage collisions could be avoided if we all an-

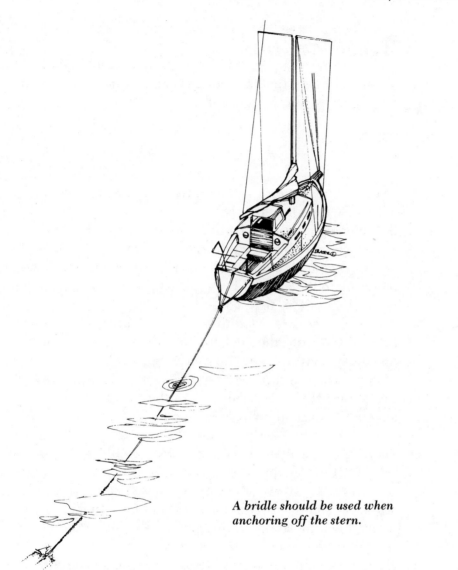

A bridle should be used when anchoring off the stern.

chored far enough away from our neighbors. But frequently there just isn't enough room. Defensive anchoring certainly will give you more security and fewer interruptions to your sleep. Just as important, it will reduce maintenance to scarred topsides, angry words and frayed tempers.

159

WEIGHING ANCHOR

When it comes time to weigh anchor, most frequently the procedure is simplicity itself.

UNDER POWER

In conditions when wind or current is not a consideration, it generally is quite practical to slowly pull the yacht towards the anchor, either by hauling manually on the rode or by winching in with the windlass or capstan.

This is considered poor seamanship by some who prefer to motor up to the anchor. Personally I see no objection to pulling on the rode in light conditions.

In more severe conditions, it certainly makes sense to bring the boat to the anchor using the engine, while simultaneously hauling in on the rode.

When you are directly over the anchor, with the rode vertical, snub the rode securely. As the yacht moves over the anchor, this usually will break it out.

Then you have only to haul it in, wash it off (along with the rode), stow it and secure it ready for sailing.

What if the anchor doesn't break out on the first pass? If powering slowly over the anchor a few times with very short scope doesn't do it, try motoring around the anchor in a small circle, keeping strain on the rode all the time. Another technique, if there is any wave action, is to snub the rode tight at the bottom of the wave and let the passing wave lift the bow and break out the anchor.

Using a buoy and trip line simplifies the procedure. Only rarely will an anchor stay put when pulled backwards by the trip line.

If the anchor is hopelessly set or severely fouled, several special tricks can be employed. We'll deal with them shortly.

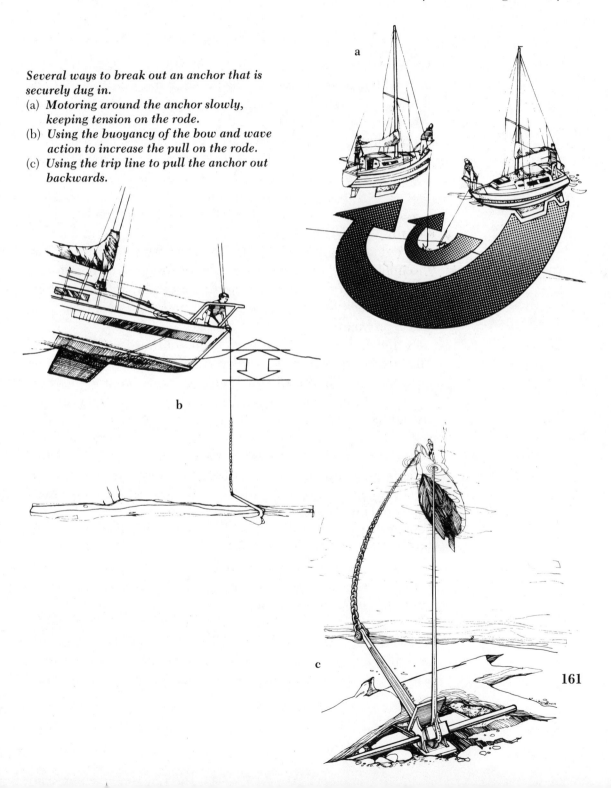

Several ways to break out an anchor that is securely dug in.

(a) *Motoring around the anchor slowly, keeping tension on the rode.*
(b) *Using the buoyancy of the bow and wave action to increase the pull on the rode.*
(c) *Using the trip line to pull the anchor out backwards.*

161

BREAKING OUT MULTIPLE ANCHORS

If more than one anchor is out, you must decide which one to lift first. Note how you will lie after the first is weighed. Usually you will lift the one to leeward first. At other times you must be sure to lift the lighter of the anchors first. These precautions are to protect you should anything go wrong. Just in case the engine should fail there is a danger you'll swing onto other yachts or hazards, leave as the last anchor the one that gives you the most protection.

I find it quite convenient to weigh the lighter anchor using the dinghy. With a trip line, this is simplicity itself. Merely row over to the buoy, haul in on the trip line and break out the anchor. It is not necessary every time to lift it into the dinghy. Secure the trip line so the anchor is off the bottom and row back to the yacht where the rode and anchor can be taken on board.

If the anchor wasn't buoyed, then you must weigh the anchor using its own rode. Pull yourself (and the dinghy) out from the yacht to the anchor, along the rode, passing the rode over the dinghy. Generally I break out the anchor merely by using the buoyancy of the dinghy and by shifting weight. For example, bring the rode over the transom, pulling the transom down to where you are just about to ship water and the rode is taut "up and down." Secure it there. Now lean back or slide your weight back towards the bow. Bow goes down, transom comes up and the anchor breaks out.

Now haul yourself back to the yacht along the rode. This generally is a very simple and seamanlike procedure, rarely practiced but often admired by other yachties who are powering thither and yon, picking up their anchors, and sometimes tangling rodes in props.

On occasion, I have found it more practical to slip the rode at the yacht, take it into the dinghy as I pull out to the anchor, weigh, then row back to the yacht. This has happened on a few occasions when someone else has swung over my rode, making it impossible to pull along the rode to the anchor and back again along the rode to the yacht.

I've also slipped the rode of one anchor, proceeded under power to pick up the other, then come around under power to pick up the first. If it was buoyed when set, the procedure is simple. A buoy can be attached to the rode before slipping. It's an easy procedure, providing no other yacht maneuvering in the anchorage tangles with your buoyed rode and/or the buoyed rode doesn't drift over some shallow sandbar or too near a yacht or other hazard to be retrieved. Think ahead! It pays.

UNDER SAIL

Many of the same techniques just described apply equally well under sail. The simplest way is to pull the boat up to the anchor, hoist the main, but leave the mainsheet slack. Be careful you don't start sailing off before you are ready. The foredeck crew must be alert and ready to snub the rode to break out the anchor smartly. Also, he or she must be ready to pay out more rode to set the anchor again should everything not go according to plan. Re-anchoring could become necessary.

If the boat remains in irons after the anchor breaks out, hoist the headsail and back it, forcing the bow off in the direction you wish to go. Once on the proper tack, the foredeck crew can haul in the anchor and stow it.

The yacht must be kept from moving too fast until the anchor is stowed, otherwise there may be damage to the hull. Once the jib is up, foredeck room is limited and extra care must be taken. Another problem is to ensure that no mud from anchor or rode gets on the sail. This is one of the hardest parts. As I noted above, the foredeck crew must be alert. Frequently other yachts are nearby, limiting maneuvering room.

Sometimes you can bring the yacht head to wind over the

163

Sailing the anchor out.

WIND

anchor, break it out, drift backwards slowly as you haul in the rode and, by swinging the tiller over to one side, control the heading, setting off under main only until the anchor is aboard and stowed securely. Conditions vary, so use the tactics that seem appropriate.

Sometimes it is better to sail the anchor out, not too difficult with a good, fast, foredeck crew and a rope rode. The main and headsail are hoisted and the yacht is tacked towards the anchor while the rode is pulled in. Sail her as fast as you can, then tack, hauling in the rode as quickly as possible. As the rode gets shorter, the tacks get shorter until finally you are sailing almost over the anchor. The scope is quite short and the anchor is snatched out, hauled in and stowed. You are away! Obviously this needs a fair bit of maneuvering room and a fair amount of practice. I doubt if it could be done with an all-chain rode.

CLEANING ANCHOR AND RODE

A deck pump is a great convenience. All too often the rode comes up covered with stinking, slimy mud. Chain is particularly bad in this respect but rope can be bad enough. Avoid getting the mud below. It can be very obnoxious.

I wish I had such a pump, but I don't and find a bucket on a lanyard works fine, even if it is less convenient. Often it takes many buckets of water to clean off the ground tackle and to swill the mud from the deck. Unless it is necessary to weigh in very difficult circumstances, the little bit of extra work with the bucket is not a problem. One person can handle the windlass and the bucket, pulling about 4′ of chain in at a time, cleaning it off, then passing it over the wildcat and into the chain locker.

Even if you have 100′ or more of chain out, it usually is only the last 20′ or so that is muddy.

In more severe conditions, one person on the windlass and

one with the bucket usually can do the job without stopping. Perhaps, some day, I'll add a pump. It would be very helpful.

If conditions permit, and you can motor ahead slowly, you can dangle the anchor (and chain) in the water to clean some of the mud off it. Do this only at low speeds. Don't let anchor or chain bang up against the hull and mar the topsides. Frankly, this practice is not good seamanship but I suspect many of us have done it on occasion.

If a whole garden of weed is dangling from the anchor, a galley butcher knife or equivalent is a good way to rid the stuff. Actually, a machete is better.

RETRIEVING A FOULED ANCHOR

There will be times when the anchor does not break out as easily as anticipated. Perhaps it is buried very deep in the mud, perhaps hooked onto coral or someone else's heavy chain or onto unknown debris. The techniques described earlier haven't produced the desired result. What now?

It would be very nice to know what is going on down there and the only way to learn this is to sight the anchor, by glass-bottom bucket, by snorkel, mask and flippers, or even by diving down to the anchor.

Sometimes, by seeing the predicament, you can free the anchor from the cable, chain, debris or whatever is holding it. Sometimes, armed with specific knowledge, you know what techniques to use. You may find it has actually broken out but has such a heavy bulk of weed or thick clay attached that it is—or merely seems—impossible to lift. In this case, all hands may be needed to get it to the surface. Once there, the heavy clay, roots or whatever can be hacked away.

Suppose it is severely fouled on old cable, chain or wreckage. Once, when wreck diving, our dive boat dropped its anchor right down the open hatch of a wooden wreck, hooking onto the coaming very thoroughly. Had the skipper insisted on trying to raise it, the wreck would have been damaged—and no good diver will damage an underwater archaeological find. There were a good number of us on board who could help, so, as he powered forward slowly to take the strain off the rode, a diver pulled the anchor out of the hatch. Problem solved.

BECUEING

If you had the foresight to anticipate a fouled anchor you could have becued it before lowering.

Becueing is simply attaching the rode to the crown of the anchor, then securing it to the shank and ring with light line.

To break the anchor free, pulling on the rode will break the light line, leaving the rode attached to the crown ready for hauling the anchor out backwards.

I do not like this system, nor do I like anchors that have an open shank. Should the wind or current reverse, or even change direction significantly, the becueing may release and the anchor could pull out accidentally. However, it is satisfactory for short periods or if you are sure the strain will not change direction.

Anchors becued so they can be retrieved more easily if fouled. Seize with light line or wire, which will break with a strong pull from above.

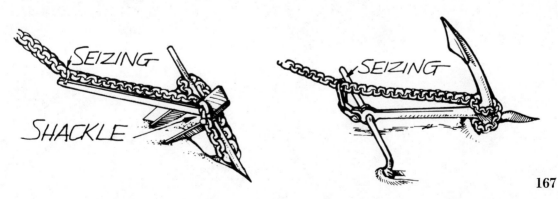

A strong trip line brought back to the yacht and winched in may lift the anchor out despite the fouling. Sometimes, short, sharp jerks on the trip line will shake off the fouling material. Whenever you're hauling the trip line, be sure the rode itself is slack, otherwise the anchor cannot come up backwards. Always make sure your trip line is strong enough to take the load.

If a lightweight is hooked onto a chain or cable, try winching it in until it is several feet or more off the bottom—the more the better. Then let the rode run out suddenly. The anchor may plane out from under the fouling material. This doesn't always work, but it is worth a try. Even the plow or Bruce has been known to come free in this manner. The anchor must be allowed to drop without restraint.

An anchor raised part way and suddenly released may plane out from under a fouling chain or cable.

Haul the fouling material to near the surface and slip a line under it to take the strain while you free the anchor.

If the fouling material can be raised near to the surface by hauling on the anchor rode, usually a line can be run under it to take the full strain. Then the anchor is lowered slightly to clear the obstacle and is winched home. It only remains to release one end of the line to let the fouling matter fall back to the bottom.

CHAIN COLLAR

A cure that almost always works is sliding a chain collar down the taut rode, right over the shank until it reaches the crown. Now slacken the rode and haul in the line attached to the

169

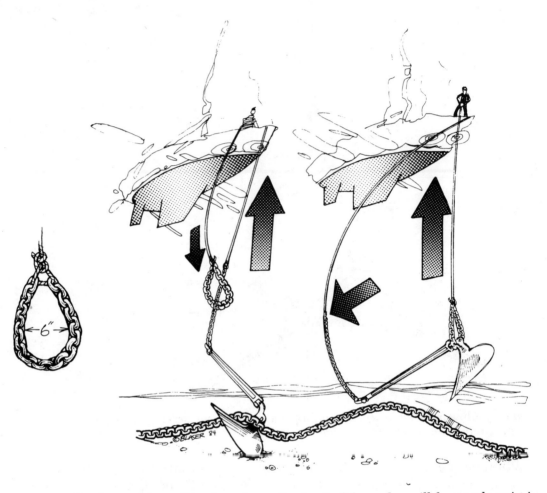

A chain collar dropped down the rode and over the shank of the anchor will frequently assist in pulling the anchor out backwards.

collar. If this doesn't work, have someone in another boat haul the line off in the direction opposite to which the anchor was set.

If all else fails, Scuba is almost certain to work. Don't abandon your anchor if it can be avoided. If you must cut and run, buoy it so you can come back for it, or so a hired Scuba diver can find it to salvage it for you.

170

DRUDGING

Some call it dredging but I prefer drudging. It is a seldom-used technique that uses anchors to maneuver a boat. It's good to know, just in case. In the early days of commercial sail it was very common practice.

It requires a current—tidal or river. In such a current, if you drift free you are out of control. Your rudder is useless. However, if you can slow the boat slightly, you create a current across the rudder and thereby a measure of control.

How to slow the drift? Drop your anchor off the bow, but with insufficient scope for it to dig in, perhaps a 2:1 ratio. The dragging anchor will slow you and create some rudder control. You can use this to steer the yacht to either side while drifting backwards.

You may be able to use the same principle to get into a berth alongside the stream, or to move away from another anchored yacht or out of the travelled channel to a safer spot —all without raising the anchor and turning on the engine.

How do you accomplish this? Presumably you have come in under sail, dropped the anchor and set it, lowered the sails and now find you want to change to another location downstream. Haul in the anchor until it starts to drag.

The current across the rudder provides control, so shorten the scope slowly until you start to drag, but leave the anchor dragging and bouncing across the bottom to slow you down.

By putting the helm over you can steer your boat to one side or the other with reasonable control (depending on the rate of current). Slow the boat by letting out more rode, increase speed by taking in rode, stop it by letting out enough for the anchor to set and bury.

Since speed is controlled by means of the rode, have someone up forward at all times. That crew, however, must be particularly cautious to keep fingers out from under the rode. Severe injury could result.

An anchor dragging from a yacht in a current permits some control and the yacht may be maneuvered over to one side or the other without engine. This is referred to as drudging.

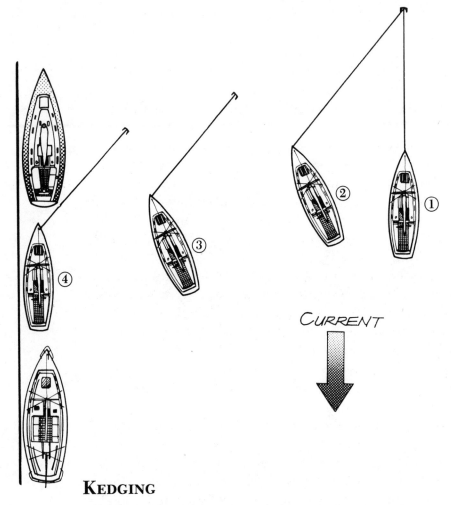

KEDGING

Kedging is the art of moving the boat from one spot to another by use of the anchors. We often refer to kedging off a grounding and this is the most common use of the technique. It can also be used to move the boat away from an obstruction, i.e., a dock, or to move the boat a considerable distance in harbor when other means of propulsion fail.

A dinghy is required and the same dinghy/anchor handling technique as described earlier.

Suppose you must get away from a berth alongside when the engine is not working and the wind is uncooperative.

Take an anchor out as far as possible by dinghy in the desired direction and set it. Now release the lines securing you to the dock while, at the same time, hauling in handsomely on the anchor rode. In this manner it is usually quite easy to get away from any obstruction such as a dock or other boats. Depending on the circumstances, you might need more than one anchor set as kedge.

When it is necessary to kedge off a grounding, depending on the severity of the grounding and whether you're on mud, sand, gravel, rocks or coral, you may find that you need far more ground tackle than you normally carry. It may require considerable improvisation and assistance from other yachts and crew.

Yachts have been salvaged from severe groundings, even stranding, by using their ground tackle, their windlass and all manner of block and tackle. Salvaging is not the subject of this book, suffice it to say that the basic technique is the same.

For the more common and simple grounding, which happens to us all too frequently, it generally is a matter of:

1) Determining the direction to deep water.

2) Taking out your heaviest possible, suitable anchor on your longest, strongest rode and setting it in the desired location using the dinghy and the procedure described earlier.

3) Reducing draft of the boat—if necessary—by taking off stores, water, heeling the boat (by putting weight on the boom or by pulling the boat over using a line from the masthead).

4) Hauling for all you're worth using the windlass and whatever blocks may be necessary to make the direction of pull suit the windlass. A capstan is easier to work with in this instance.

If you have enough crew, set two anchors as kedges—one on the windlass and one hauled by hand or by block and tackle, or by use of a sheet winch.

Another form of kedging, very common in the days of our seafaring ancestors, was used to move the ship into harbor in a calm, or perhaps against a weak current.

Two anchors, two long rodes and one, strong, tireless crewmember in a dinghy are all that are required.

You are anchored with anchor #1 on a short scope. Put anchor #2 into the dinghy, take it out ahead as far as the rode will permit, drop it and set it. Now haul up to anchor #1, break it out and raise it to the bow roller, then haul up as close as you can get to #2 without breaking it out.

While this is being done, anchor #1 is put into the dinghy and rowed out ahead as far as the rode will permit, dropped and set. Anchor #2 is broken out, raised and put into the dinghy. Now that tireless crewman again rows off ahead while the yacht is pulled up to anchor #1.

The yacht never needs to come to a stop, but it can be very tiring work, something you won't want to do very often. It worked for our great grandfathers who had to kedge much larger ships than ours. It still works for us, though you may find your tireless crewman unwilling to crew for you again.

It's a sort of leapfrogging procedure, "leap-anchoring" if you prefer, and worth knowing. It might get you out of difficulties someday. It's much more efficient than towing the yacht with the dinghy.

HURRICANE ANCHORING

It generally is considered safer for a well-found and adequately crewed yacht to weather a major storm well offshore than to do so at anchor. The principal dangers are not so much the wind and the waves as the hard stuff around the edges of any anchorage, from other boats, docks, ships and from flying debris and the like.

Storm surges, abnormal high tides and waves frequently lift yachts up and over the docks they are tied to, sometimes impaling them on the pilings. Thus boats left tied to docks are almost certain to suffer major damage or even be a total loss.

But few sailors are willing to head off to sea when a hurricane threatens. Most boats are not suitable for weathering such storms at sea. If your boat is insured, take all seamanlike precautions, including hauling the boat if you are able, and wait out the storm onshore.

If your boat cannot be hauled out and trucked well inland before the storm hits, the next best choice is to find a location where it can be secured with lines in all four directions. In tropical waters, a mangrove swamp makes an excellent locale for weathering a hurricane.

If possible, find a hurricane hole offering excellent holding and good protection from the winds in all directions. Moorings are not to be trusted unless you are sure of them and have inspected all that is underwater, chain, shackles, etc., and know just what is buried down there in the mud. They frequently are set too close together to provide adequate swinging room for the most severe storm conditions. Use of proper ground tackle usually is preferred.

Particular care must be paid to details such as shock-absorbing snubbers, proper anti-chafe guard and, of course, extra strong and extra long rodes.

As to the anchor itself, the most secure arrangement, presuming you have selected suitable anchors and rode, and they are well set and dug in, is two in tandem. This is preferred to two anchors on separate rodes, set a few degrees apart.

However, the winds may come from any and all directions and the only way to prepare for this contingency is to set three anchors 120° apart, or four 90° apart (See figure, page 146). All should be on long rodes, secured together, preferably at a swivel. If the anchors are set too close together, should they drag—as they are certainly apt to do to some extent—they may end up in a tangle. Or, the rodes may tangle and end up in nothing more than a mass, acting as a weight but not as an anchor. Two rodes should connect from the swivel to two separate points at the bow of the yacht. Dive to inspect all the anchors if possible, to ensure that they are well dug in.

I won't comment on the subject of whether you should seek safety ashore or stay on board. Should you stay on board, and I would comment that the safety of personnel is more important than that of the boat, check the chafe guard frequently. Dodging into the storm is not apt to be much help unless you have a very powerful engine and a lot of fuel. But it can't hurt. Make sure sheets or other lines don't wash off the deck and foul the prop. (A good hurricane survival story appears in *Sail*'s February, 1984 issue. The 43-foot ketch *Redhawk* survived a major hurricane in the South Pacific by dodging into the storm after two anchor rodes chafed through. All other yachts in the anchorage (except one) were washed ashore. It's good reading.)

Be prepared to fend off other vessels whose anchors snatch out or lines chafe through, and who drag down onto your yacht.

This short piece is not intended to be a full discussion of how to weather a hurricane at anchor. Hurricanes come in all degrees of severity. There are cases where no possible ground tackle that a yacht might carry will save it.

AVOIDING ANCHORING ACCIDENTS

Possibly no other activity associated with cruising is so apt to cause as much injury as anchor handling. I suspect only galley duty is as dangerous.

A fast-moving rope running through one's hands can cause a burn as severe as picking up a hot iron rod. Avoid touching a running line with bare hands or bare feet. Always veer out and haul rode (if by hand) with a turn taken first around a cleat, bitt or Samson post. Wear gloves.

Chain is even worse when it gets out of control. Your hands

may not get burned but they can be cut or badly bruised. Even ordinary work gloves offer inadequate protection, here.

Even worse is getting your fingers caught between rope and hawse hole or chock, between chain and roller or in the gypsy. Many a sailor has required stitches or even amputation of fingers for this reason alone. It happens to the neophyte and even to those with long years of experience, such as Eric Hiscock.

Then, of course, there is the danger of hernia or back injury from straining to lift and manhandle a heavy anchor. In this way alone a windlass pays for itself over and over again.

Without doubt the worst hazard is getting one's feet caught in a running rope or chain. Flesh can be cut severely, bones can be broken and crew can be pulled overboard.

Take the case of the late Alain Colas, a widely-known French sailor with a great deal of experience. He was bringing his trimaran, *Manuereva,* into the port of La Trinité sur Mer after a pleasant sail with friends. The mainsail jammed and wouldn't come down. Only one way to stop the boat.

Colas left the helm, rushed forward and let go the anchor. The 90-pound anchor went to the bottom instantly while the inboard end of the chain cable made a loop in the air and wound itself around Colas' foot. He was in the hospital for six months. His leg, although very badly mangled, did not require amputation. He suffered severely for many more months but eventually was back sailing again.

It always pays to plan ahead. And everyone who handles ground tackle must be thoroughly familiar with anchoring procedures and safety issues. I don't like to see chain ranged out on deck nor rope flaked out because of what can happen if either gets out of control.

RAFTING AT ANCHOR

In suitable weather conditions, rafting is a pleasant way to get together after a day of sailing. Suitable conditions means almost total calm, minimal current and negligible action.

Usually, the largest boat with the heaviest ground tackle sets its anchor first and makes ready to welcome its neighbors. Remember that rafting creates heavier strains than normal and adequate precautions should be taken in selecting anchors, using high scope ratio and ensuring a proper anchor set.

Each boat, as it arrives, should have its biggest fenders secured alongside where they will give maximum protection to the anchored boat (usually the widest part). If possible, set fenders at various heights. Bow and stern lines plus spring lines fore and aft should be secured between the two boats. Use your own fenders and lines when you join the group. Each newcomer should do the same. This makes things a great deal less confusing when it comes time to break up the raft.

Rafting requires good fenders and spring lines. Be sure masts are staggered to prevent damage to rigging.

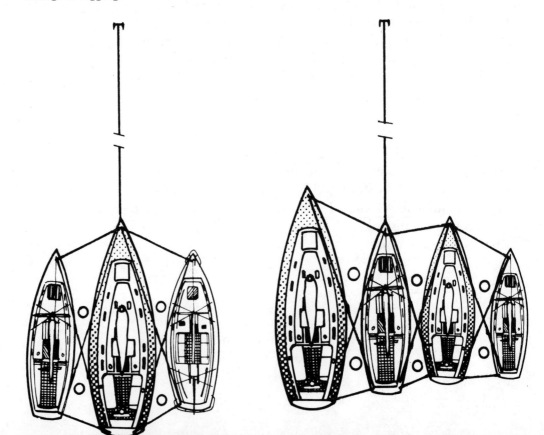

178

The raft should be kept balanced, with the same number of boats tied on each side of the anchored boat. A large boat on one side may be balanced by two smaller boats on the other. Make sure the spreaders and rigging will not hit one another. Move boats forward or aft slightly to stagger the masts.

Do not set anchors from more than one boat if any possibility exists whatsoever of wind or current change. Serious ground tackle tangles may result.

Never leave rafted boats unattended. This includes leaving the raft anchored all night, even if crews are sleeping aboard. A sudden squall could cause pandemonium, a jumble of tangled lines (including some around props) and battered topsides. If your boat mars the one to which you have rafted, you could be held liable.

Remember the skipper/owner is responsible for his yacht and his crew. At times the socializing and drinking gets out of hand. It may be difficult, but the skipper must remain sober enough to handle his boat safely in any emergency. In the event of a squall, an anchorage full of drunken sailors charging about in all directions is a pitiful and disgusting— even frightening—sight.

If you prefer crowds to solitude, then raft instead of anchor by yourself. However, take the necessary precautions and be prepared for any possible consequences.

HAND SIGNALS

Learning a few hand signals to be used between helmsman and foredeck crew is a mark of seamanship that will be appreciated by all who watch you from their cockpit or the club verandah. They are equally useful while anchoring, weighing and docking.

Most of us have watched the person on the foredeck try to communicate with the helmsman by shouting excitedly over his shoulder. Meanwhile the helmsman, who can't understand a word being said, is getting nervous and frustrated. It pays off in fewer accidents and fewer angry exchanges to learn hand signals.

There need be no standardization. What works on one boat isn't necessarily right on another. Note that the foredeck hand must be in command of the anchoring procedure.

I like signals that can be seen from a distance, even in fog or drizzle. Signals using only the fingers may not be distinguishable. The signals I suggest all involve motion and/or the entire arm. The signalling arm should be out to one side, never out in front where it may be hidden from the helmsman's view.

1. A hand (and arm) pointing to port or starboard indicates the direction to go, the direction the anchor line is tending, or the direction to the mooring buoy.

2. As the anchor is approached, to short stay, the arm points nearly straight down.

3. When breaking out the anchor, the hand is raised, to one side, and moved up and down to indicate a vertical rode.

4. The hand out with the thumb erect and still moving up and down indicates the anchor is broken out.

5. The arm is held erect when the anchor is cock-a-bill and it is o.k. to proceed.

6. Forward power needed: Point the index finger up and describe a series of small circles. If more power needed, increase the speed of the signals.

7. Reverse power needed: Point the index finger down and describe circles as before.

8. Put the engine in neutral: Extend the hand to one side, palm down and moving horizontally slowly, like a safe call in baseball.

9. Cut engine. Hand to one side. Pantomime the act of turning off the key.

All these signals require only one hand. The other is available for holding onto the forestay for handling the anchor rode, or whatever.

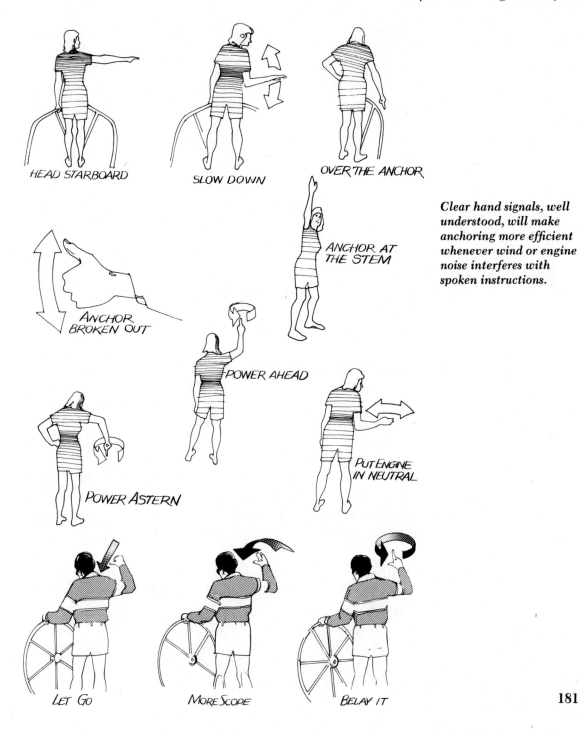

HEAD STARBOARD

SLOW DOWN

OVER THE ANCHOR

ANCHOR AT THE STEM

ANCHOR BROKEN OUT

POWER AHEAD

POWER ASTERN

PUT ENGINE IN NEUTRAL

LET GO

MORE SCOPE

BELAY IT

Clear hand signals, well understood, will make anchoring more efficient whenever wind or engine noise interferes with spoken instructions.

Here are a few signals the helmsman might need to give the foredeck man.

1. Let go: An overhead, thumbs-down motion.
2. More scope: An overhead waving to forward.
3. Secure or snub: A circular signal like wrapping the line around a bollard or bitt.

Become expert at using signals like these instead of shouting. You'll receive many congratulations on your boat-handling techniques and will enjoy your cruise much more.

However, it is obvious that on a small boat or in benign conditions, the spoken word is not only adequate but preferable. Hand-signals must never replace good seamanship, such as when the crew must use one hand to operate the anchor windlass, the other for personal security. Where does he get the other with which to signal? There are times and places for both methods.

KNOW THE PROPER KNOTS

Knowing proper ground tackle and proper anchoring, berthing and mooring techniques, may prove worthless if lines part because your knots slip. Half a dozen or so knots will meet at least 90% of your needs adequately.

The *fisherman's bend*, also called the *anchor bend*, is probably the most common knot used to tie a line to an anchor ring. The *anchor bowline* is better. It consists of a standard bowline with an extra turn around the anchor ring. A bowline on the bight is best of all. *The Ashley Book of Knots* (pages 194 and 195) shows several ways to form this knot.

The bowline is an excellent knot for securing to a bollard or piling.

Many, however, prefer the *clove hitch* because it seems easier to do and is excellent, providing there is tension on the line. A surging boat, which is adding and releasing tension frequently, may cause the clove hitch to release inad-

ANCHOR BEND

ANCHOR BOWLINE

vertently. Adding a half hitch to the standing part will prevent this from happening.

An alternate knot for securing to a piling is the *round turn and two half hitches.* It also is good for hanging fenders on the lifeline or from the handrails. Note the distinct difference between this and the fisherman's bend. Don't use this one for attaching a line to your anchor.

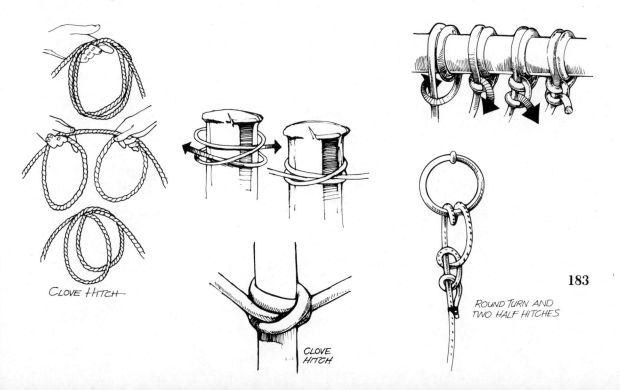

CLOVE HITCH

CLOVE HITCH

ROUND TURN AND TWO HALF HITCHES

183

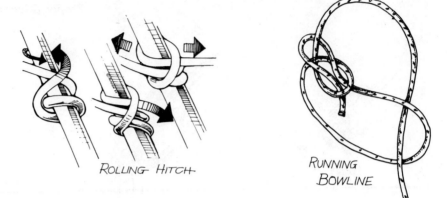

ROLLING HITCH

RUNNING BOWLINE

A *running bowline* is good for the large loop when you try to lasso a bollard or piling.

The *rolling hitch* is used when the strain on the line essentially is parallel to the object, rope or chain to which it is tied. For example, it is applicable when attaching a nylon snubber to an anchor chain.

If lines are to be attached for a long period, such as when the yacht is unattended, it pays to seize the free end of the line to the standing part.

When you must join two ropes of different sizes, such as in extending an anchor rode or kedging warp, the *sheet bend* is the most common knot. A more secure knot is the *double sheet bend* and is only slightly more difficult, so I prefer it.

SHEET BEND

DOUBLE SHEET BEND

Attaching to a cleat.

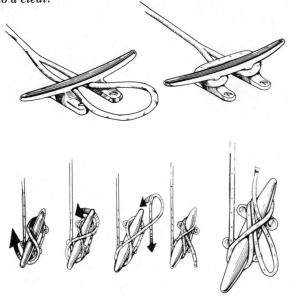

Mooring lines using long splices to form end loops are very easy to secure to large cleats with open bases.

If the cleat does not have an open base, take a full turn around the base, then a *figure-of-eight* turn, ending with a half hitch. Adding more turns or more than one half hitch does not add to the security and makes it more difficult to release.

Attaching to a bollard or bitts.

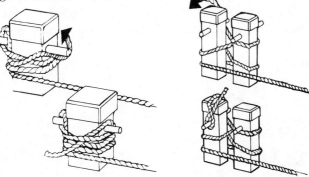

185

CHAPTER 4

Mooring And Docking

Without doubt, docking and undocking activities produce more scarred topsides than any other boating activity.

At the same time, they produce more ludicrous situations, more humor, more frayed nerves, more displays of sarcasm and even temper.

Des Sleightholme, a man full of wisdom and humor, told this docking story in the September, 1983 issue of *Yachting Monthly:*

> The husband was at the yacht's helm and his wife was forward as the yacht approached the jetty. "Drop two fenders over the side and throw the heaving line to that chap," the husband commanded. She did exactly that. It's my guess she was settling an old score as she watched those fenders drift away.

The story points out the crying need for the skipper to plan ahead and make sure his crew knows and understands their part in the docking maneuver.

186

I believe, emphatically, that the most agile and physically able crew member should handle the duties that require greater activity and strength. There is an old expression though, that says it is the owner's privilege to run his vessel aground. Most owners prefer to be at the helm when any chance exists of close encounters with docks, mooring buoys and such.

Among the first things a novice must learn is the way his boat handles in mooring and berthing situations. How much way will she carry in various conditions of wind and current? How does she handle at very slow speeds under sail? Under power? How does she behave when backing down? Will she respond to the skipper or does she behave with a will of her own?

Small boats fitted with outboards are much easier to handle in reverse than are heavier yachts with inboards, because the direction of thrust can readily be controlled by turning the outboard.

Most sailboats, when backing down, will turn their stern into the wind because of the higher windage up forward. This is a factor you must get used to.

Learn to handle your boat in the vicinity of docks without having to rely on shoreside help. Many times marina dockhands are not as competent as one might like them to be. Frequently they are students hired for the season. Learn to be independent and take the responsibility for docking and undocking yourself.

Remember, though, there is a great deal of weight being moved around. Don't get hands or feet caught between the dock and the rubrail. Feet don't make good fenders.

CHOOSING YOUR BERTH

Frequently there is little choice of berths available. Our marinas often are overcrowded and you must take the berth assigned to you. The only alternatives are to anchor off, or to seek another marina or club. If you are renting by the season you probably have your docking lines already attached to rings or cleats, perhaps even fendering material all along the dockside. This certainly makes the operation very much easier.

When you do have a choice of berths, here are a few things you should look for:

1. Naturally, a strong, well-maintained dock is highly desirable. You don't want one that is a hazard for those walking to and from the boat, nor one from which spikes and other jagged bits of metal project, all ready to take chunks out of your gelcoat.

2. If in tidal waters, a floating dock is usually much preferred to fixed, barnacle-encrusted pilings. Sometimes that is all that's available. It shouldn't be necessary to point out that you need sufficient depth of water at low tide. I've been fooled by marina dockhands who have assured me there was plenty of water, only to find my keel in the mud during the night.

3. Ease of access and escape for the boat. When you come in off the open sea, tired and hungry, that dock looks like a symbol of security and comfort. Could it become a trap if the wind shifts and a storm makes up? Have you room to maneuver and get out again safely under conditions that make the berth untenable?

4. How well is the dock protected from wind, waves and current, from all directions? Could a severe swell make it very uncomfortable?

In company with several others, I spent much of a stormy night, several years ago at a marina on Lake Champlain out in the driving rain. The storm was causing the floating dock to break up and we had to move many boats to safer spots at other docks. That was a good experience in warping, for many boats had been left unattended by their owners so, of course, their engines were not available.

5. Amenities. You may be seeking fuel, water, electricity, even telephone and cable T.V. You may want a place to park the car at dockside. You may need showers, laundry, shopping and access to bus, train or plane.

Very important is the requirement for all crew and guests to get on and off the yacht conveniently and safely. At first thought, it seems so obvious, but, at times you may secure to dock or pilings at deck level and wake up next morning to find that same dock 8' or more above deck level. Where did you stow your extension ladder? Don't expect crewmembers to climb a slimy, barnacle-coated piling or to walk along a pier of rotten planks.

BERTHING EQUIPMENT

One of the greatest mistakes one sees in our marinas is use of inadequate lines and fenders. I fail to understand why anyone invests $10,000 or $100,000, or whatever, in a boat and next to nothing to protect it from damage. The use of excessively light mooring lines and toy fenders is all too common. For a small fraction of 1% of the value of the boat, per year, you can have the best of lines and fenders.

Exactly what you need will vary with boat size and tie up conditions. Here, for example, is what I would consider minimum for a boat of 25 to 35' L.O.A.

Four ½" nylon lines, 50' long
Two ½" nylon lines 100' long
Three air fenders, 8" diameter, preferably 10 or 12"
One fender board 6 to 8' long. Two are better
Several rubber snubbers
Anti-chafe gear
Heaving line

Fenders should be large, strong and plentiful. For mooring against pilings or rough, uneven walls, a fenderboard is essential. Watch for chafe of any ropes left exposed as shown here.

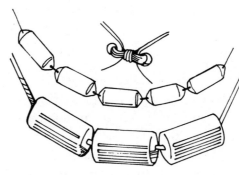

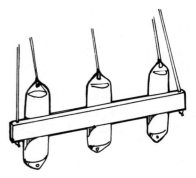

In tidal waters, or if you are transitting canals, you will need more lines and longer lines and bigger fenders, perhaps canvas-covered tires or burlap sacks filled with straw.

You may get away with lighter lines and/or shorter lines but I'm presuming you will be mooring from time to time against long docks and finger docks, between pilings, and that your boat may be subjected to varieties of weather.

I'm also presuming, because we discussed it earlier in this text, that your yacht is equipped with strong, reinforced-back, mooring cleats and chocks, two of each at the bow, one of each at each quarter and preferably one of each amidships on each side.

Amidships chocks and cleats have a value far above their cost to any boat that must be maneuvered extensively around docks. Unfortunately, they are not found very often on stock boats.

THE HEAVING LINE

One of the seaman's skills that every boatowner should acquire early in the game and teach to his or her crew, is the art of making up and throwing a heaving line properly.

Some appear to have an amazing and wonderful trust in the Almighty, for they will pick up a coil of line and toss it in the air, expecting it to untangle itself and sail off in the right direction. It just doesn't work that way.

Like so many skills, it does work when you know how, and it's so easy to learn, so why not?

For our purposes here, no special line is needed. Three strand or braid will work, though the latter is somewhat better. A suitable line is 50' of ⅜" or ½" nylon. Too light a line is difficult to throw to windward. However if you make up a ¼" line and fit it with a monkey fist, it serves well when used to pull across a heavier line. When docking, however, rarely is there time for this.

191

Do not try the impossible. Wait until you are as close as you can safely get. Throwing it too soon, or before you have it properly coiled, usually will result in a splash in the water between you and the dock. Don't try to heave too much of the mass of rope. Fifty feet of line is not necessary when only 10′ separates you from the dock.

It is best to first secure the bitter end to a deck cleat. Take the coil in your left hand (if you are right-handed), shift half to your right hand and with an open, sidearm motion of the right arm heave the coil and simultaneously open the left hand only enough so that the line in it can pay out and follow the coil through the air.

Do not throw the line directly at the recipient. He is not going to be very happy to receive a bundle of wet line in the face or even the chest. Throw it over and past him but within reach.

It is an easy skill to acquire and one that will pay off in many ways.

Frequently when you must secure to a piling, whether alongside a dock or off the quarter, it must be done very quickly. Otherwise you may suffer being blown off, hard against the dock or against a neighbor.

A bowline with a very large loop, or a large loop spliced into the line, or in fact, any loop that quickly can be dropped over the piling and pulled tight can save the day, as well as save face.

Berthing between pilings is a common situation and difficult for the uninitiated to accomplish without embarrassment. If you have a crew who can help, here is one way to do it.

Have the crew take a line forward, from the stern chock, outside everything. The line should be fitted with a large loop as above and the skipper should bring the boat in to the berth alongside the upwind or upcurrent outer piling. The crew can slip the loop over the piling ready for the skipper to pull it tight from the cockpit.

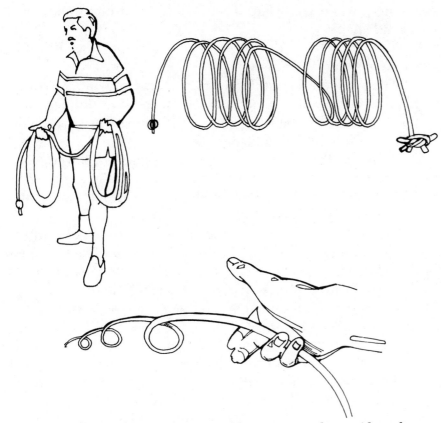

The ability to heave a line with reasonable accuracy and to avoid tangles is a talent every crewmember should acquire.

A boat hook may be necessary for the crew forward. At low tide some of the pilings can be mighty high.

If you can learn to play cowboy and lasso the piling, you will receive accolades from many an attentive audience.

There are several ways of doing this, perhaps the simplest comes from Dale Nouse, who tells me he has captured a couple of hundred pilings.

"Take a doubled length of line, coil as usual and throw the bight end at the piling. If any part of the line lands on top of the piling, a simple twitch right or left drops the bight around the piling. Further, this system gives you a doubled line, a

193

big help when you want to retrieve it, in case of trouble or when leaving."

For the cowboy technique you need a running bowline on a line of some ⅜" diameter.

Make a noose about 18" in diameter. Hold the bowline loosely in your left hand and pull more line through the bowline making about 10 loops of the noose in your right hand, each about 18" in diameter.

Throw, in the same, open, sweeping manner, toward the piling, all the 10 loops in your right hand, at the same time permitting the running bowline to leave your left hand, but don't let go of the standing part.

The noose will open up in the air and the running bowline will run along the line. It will require some practice undoubtedly, but believe me, it does work. With more practice, perhaps even I can make it work most of the time.

Another difficult situation, and a technique I learned in order to cope with it involves buoys instead of pilings.

Each yacht at my yacht club in Toronto, the Queen City Yacht Club, is berthed bow to the seawall with lines from each quarter to two car wheels and inflated tires, secured to heavy weights on the bottom.

As we back down out of our mooring space, we drop these stern lines on to the tires as carefully as possible. On returning to the berth, the crew on the foredeck picks up the two bow lines with a boat hook and the skipper or crew in the cockpit picks up the two stern lines. Floats are added to these lines and, in most cases, a piece of floating polypropylene joins them all together.

When conditions are benign, it is a relatively simple matter, accomplished with little difficulty or excitement but with dexterous use of the boat hooks.

In rougher weather, it is another matter and at low speeds you can be blown quickly to one side or the other. Then we welcome neighbors standing ready to lend a hand, to fend off and protect their own topsides.

APPROACHING THE BERTH

As they say, "now comes the crunch." Hopefully there will be no crunch. Approach the dock slowly, but always under control. Never lose steerage way! If under power, remember a yacht's brakes are notoriously ineffective.

Be independent. Don't count on dockhands, even though it is very nice to have someone on the dock lend a hand with your lines. Particularly when the weather is not cooperating, a friend on the docks can help fend off and keep you out of difficulties. But one never knows the expertise of the stranger who comes forward so willingly to lend a hand. He may take your bow line and quickly make it fast before your boat stops moving. This happened to me once and the bow swung in to hit the concrete dock while the stern swung out. I had no fender right at the bow so the topsides received some new scratches.

Have your fenders and lines ready. The skipper should already have made a note of the dock height and instructed the crew how far down to hang the fenders or the fender-board. This must be done early. One extra-large fender should be kept in reserve to slip in at the last moment where and if needed.

Have everything ready before approaching the dock and a crewman prepared to hop ashore to secure the yacht.

195

Your crew should be properly stationed but they should know enough not to block the skipper's line of vision as he approaches the dock.

Determine whether wind or current will take charge. Always approach against this force if at all possible. Never approach with it.

If the wind or current is forcing you down onto the dock, broadside, bring your yacht dead in the water several feet out from where you intend to secure, and let it be forced down gently.

Yacht (a) *has come to a standstill a few feet from the dock and will be blown against it gently. Yacht* (b) *has wind blowing her away from the dock and must get lines ashore promptly. Yacht* (c) *has secured temporarily to the end of a finger pier and may be easily warped in alongside on either side of the pier. Yacht* (d) *performed a dangerous landing, coming in to a dock, downwind. However, once secured, she may be warped around on either side.*

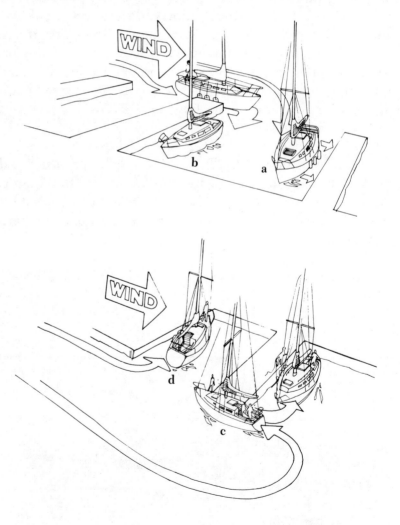

196

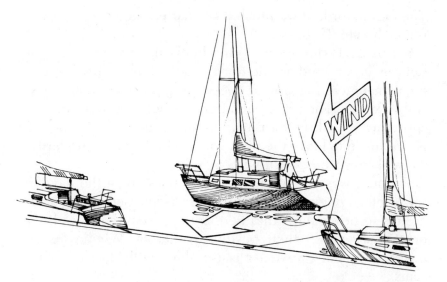

If the force is away from the dock, come in fairly sharp and get lines ashore quickly, before you are forced away.

At times it is best to secure at the end of a finger pier where you have better control, then warp her around into your slip.

Usually, the best line to secure first is a midship spring line. Either take it ashore, pass it to a helper, or lasso a piling, bollard or cleat on the dock as you approach.

An after spring, once secured, will help pull the boat alongside without changing direction appreciably.

USING SPRING LINES AND WARPS

Once you are berthed, spring lines are used to prevent excessive movement of the boat either ahead or astern.

The principal springs are forward bow spring, forward midship spring, forward quarter spring, aft bow spring, aft midship spring and aft quarter spring. Usually only one forward and one aft spring are used at any time.

The naming is important. A forward spring is one that leads forward from the boat and an aft spring one that leads aft.

The other word, bow, midship or quarter, indicates where it is attached to the boat.

Springing is the use of spring lines, along with engine or sail power, or wind or tide to position or move a boat. Warping is maneuvering around docks using warps only, and possibly a kedge. The principal difference between warping and springing is that, in warping, neither engine nor sail power is employed to move the boat. In view of the great similarity, we will cover the two subjects together.

Warping was an extremely important skill in the days of sail (before engines), and our forefathers used these techniques to bring ships into berths, to reverse their headings or otherwise shift their position in harbor. Windlasses on board were put to extensive use along with dockside capstans.

Proper use of warps and springs is still a valuable skill for the seaman of today.

In addition to securing the boat when lying alongside, springs can be invaluable in docking and undocking exercises. Preferably the springs should be attached to the boat using proper chocks and cleats. Attaching to a stanchion is a very poor substitute. At times, on a light yacht, a snatch block may be used, attached to a toerail. The spring line is brought through the snatch block and then forward or aft to a cleat.

Use of a snatch block and line to the cockpit is a very effective way for a singlehander to deal with springs. It is as easy to heave a line to the dockhand from the cockpit as from amidships.

A spring line from the bow or stern usually is very unsatisfactory when coming in to a dock. The former will tend to pull the bow in toward the dock, often causing damage, while the latter will do the same with the stern.

With an after spring attached amidships and forward power applied, the boat will be drawn sideways in toward the dock. The rudder is used to keep the boat parallel and, in calm conditions, the boat can be held this way indefinitely while

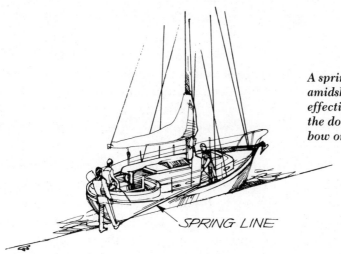

A spring line from a cleat amidships and leading aft is most effective in stopping the boat at the dock without swinging the bow or stern in.

SPRING LINE

you attach bow and stern lines and otherwise make all lines secure, in a calm and leisurely fashion. Only then need you shut down the engine.

If you lack a midship chock and cleat, try using the other cleats but do it slowly. You may, by experiment, come up with a technique that works for you. More often than not, you will end up adding or devising some arrangement for securing amidships.

As you approach the dock, with all lines and fenders ready, if you can lasso the right piling or bollard, all well and good. If you must heave your line to a stranger on the dock, have him secure the line to the piling, bollard or cleat of your choice. You should haul in and secure from your own boat, where you are in control.

Take up the slack and put the spring under tension with forward power, keeping light tension on your spring line until all other lines are secure.

In all docking and undocking operations, take your time. Note wind and current. Know your own and your crew's capabilities. Don't let anyone (either your own crew or a dockhand) rush you into doing something for which you are not prepared. Plan an escape route if possible. Should anything go wrong and you damage your own boat or another, it is you, not the dockhand, who is responsible.

Always be prepared with an alternate plan. What if you put

on power and the dockhand's knot doesn't hold, or the dock cleat pulls out? Have you thought out what you would do? All crew must keep their hands and feet out from between boat and dock. Have an extra (large) fender handy that can be inserted anywhere it may be needed.

Practice how to perform the docking operations single-handed. Have all your lines ready in advance, bring the mid-ship spring line back to the cockpit. Rig fenders and spring lines on both sides if you are not sure to which side you will be docking. Fore and aft breast lines may be rigged later if the spring is properly used.

It pays to have boathooks handy, both forward and in the cockpit. In some situations your lines are left on the dock when you go out for a sail. A boathook permits these to be picked up and secured to cleats, at least temporarily, without ever leaving the boat.

Getting away from a dock usually is simpler, if only because you are starting from a stationary position.

Let's look at how you might get out (forward) from a tight berth alongside, port side to. We'll neglect wind and current in this instance.

Put tension on your aft bow spring by applying power forward at slow revs. Take off all lines except the aft spring. Now, with rudder well to port, the thrust will push your stern out and your bow in. In this case, depending on how far it is necessary to put the stern out, the spring may be attached amidships or well forward, even to a forward cleat. Watch those fenders! The bow will swing in as the stern swings out. Once the stern is out far enough to clear all other yachts, slip the spring off and, in reverse, pull away from the dock, then proceed forward. (A forward spring line and engine in reverse will let you bring the bow out in a similar manner.)

Should it be necessary to reverse direction in order to pull away in the direction opposite to that in which you were berthed, continuing to power forward with an aft spring secured to the bow will continue to pull the stern around, away

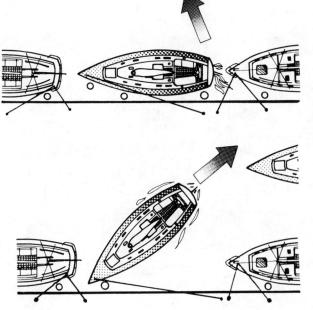

Powering against an after bow spring swings the bow in and the stern out. Now slip the spring and back down into the clear.

from the dock. Be careful you don't damage your stem or dolphin striker. Having someone on the dock to hold you off a few inches can be a big help in this maneuver. When you swing around until the bow is almost at a right angle to the dock, reverse the rudder and put the engine in reverse. You will end up well clear of other boats and heading in the opposite direction.

We have been talking of using a single spring line looped over a pier cleat or bollard. An alternative that is particularly

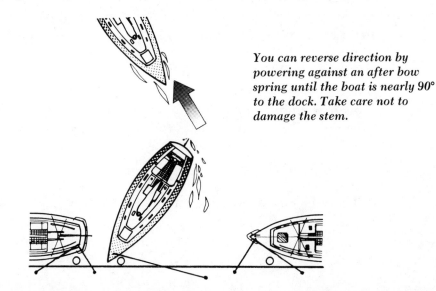

You can reverse direction by powering against an after bow spring until the boat is nearly 90° to the dock. Take care not to damage the stem.

201

By doubling the spring line or the last line to be cast off, you can pull away from the dock, then release one end and pull in the other.

useful when getting away from a dock is to loop your line over that dockside fastening and doubling the end back to the yacht. Then, as you complete the operation, you let go one end from on deck, haul in the other end and stow the line. Loose lines have a knack of catching in cracks on the dock, around themselves, or snagging on almost invisible objects. Remember, too, that loose lines in the water are subject to a great "magnetic" pull from the prop and almost certain to find their way there with disastrous results. Never let lines drag over the side!

Commercial boats make daily use of springs to maneuver around docks. It is interesting to see the larger ships being moved around using springs and currents.

There will be times when you cannot see with certainty how you are going to get out of a tight slip in a strong wind or current without damaging neighboring yachts—or your own—and creating pandemonium.

There is nothing unseamanlike in seeking help. Take lines

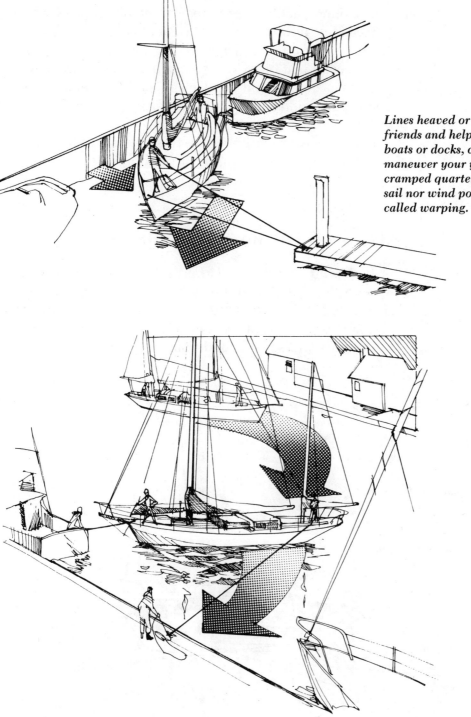

Lines heaved or taken to friends and helpers on other boats or docks, can help you maneuver your yacht in cramped quarters with neither sail nor wind power. This is called warping.

203

out to other yachts where they can be of help and wherever you can find a cooperative crewman. You may be able to walk the lines around or perhaps use the dinghy.

The combination of these *warping lines,* with or without your own engine and rudder can save you embarrassment and expense and add to the respect you get from the dockside critics.

By using warping lines like this you can shift berths, reverse direction, change slips or perform many other maneuvers.

SECURING THE BOAT IN ITS BERTH

A boat well secured in its berth will have forward and aft springs, forward and aft breast lines and possibly a bow line and a stern line. As the latter are functioning as spring lines to some extent, they are not essential in calm conditions.

Of course, in severe conditions, more lines may be added

A well-secured yacht will have a bow line (1) a stern line (2), possibly crossed to the outside as shown, two spring lines (3) and (4) and two breast lines (5) and (6).

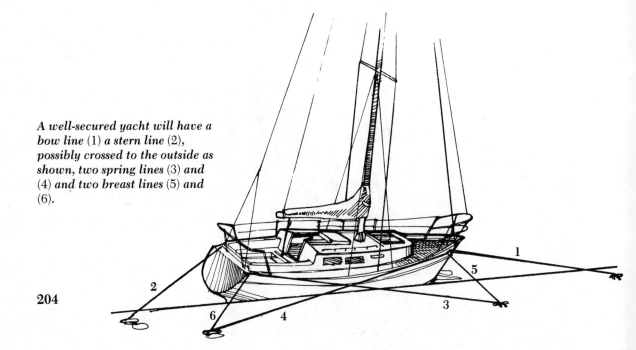

204

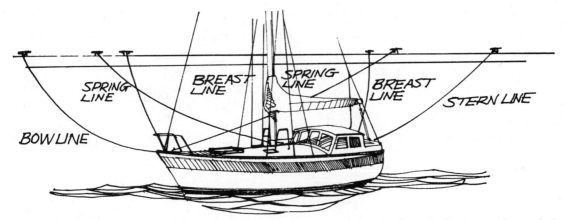

In large tidal range such as this, it is necessary to keep someone on board, as the lines must be tended almost constantly. Be sure to use chafe guard where lines abraid against the harbor wall.

and/or lines doubled. Do not forget that rubber snubbers may be inserted in the lines to take the severe shocks if there is much wave action.

Long springs are an essential ingredient when coping with rise or fall of tides. The longer the lines the greater the tidal range that can be handled. At times spring lines are crossed at the stern to provide greater length. Remember to check your mooring lines as the tide constantly rises and falls. And don't forget to use chafe-guard wherever the ropes are subject to wear, on the boat or on the dock.

Rubber snubbers in the mooring lines will help keep the boat at rest, reducing quick motion caused by swells and passing boats.

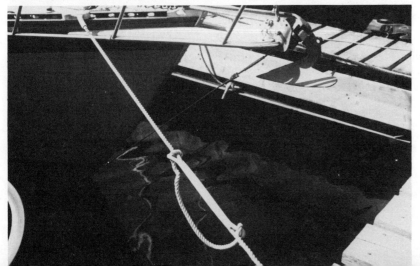

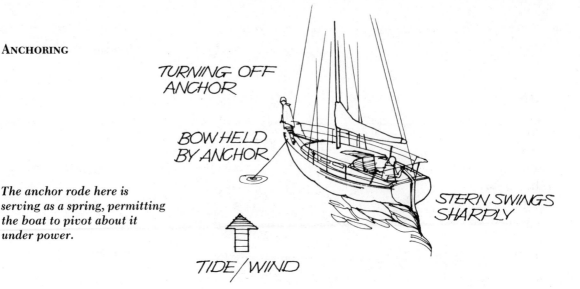

TURNING OFF
ANCHOR

BOW HELD
BY ANCHOR

STERN SWINGS
SHARPLY

TIDE/WIND

*The anchor rode here is
serving as a spring, permitting
the boat to pivot about it
under power.*

The anchor rode also can be employed as a spring to turn your boat if that is necessary in tight quarters.

The anchor should be down and dug in. Put the rudder hard over with engine gently forward and the boat will pivot around the anchor, turning 180° or more or less as needed. Another way to reverse direction at anchor is to bring a line from the stern cleat, forward to the mooring or anchor line. When the anchor or mooring line is released, the boat will change its heading. By definition, since the engine is not used, this is more warping than springing.

This method frequently is used at anchor to bring the boat at right angles to swells and reduce the rolling. At a mooring it can help you get away under sail from a crowded mooring. You can head the boat so the wind catches the sails on the desired tack, then drop off the lines and get underway.

*Using a spring line at a buoy
to change the angle at which
the vessel lies at mooring, or to
enable it to get away on a
preferred tack.*

SPRINGING OF BUOY

WIND/TIDE

HEAD FALLS OFF
AS HEAD LINE IS
VEERED. STERN
REMAINS SECURED
TO BUOY

MAINTAINING YOUR LINES

To make a coil with three-strand line, take the line in your left hand and with a sweeping motion of the right hand feed the line into the left in clockwise loops. Give each loop a slight clockwise twist to cause the loops to fall into a neat coil. This is important; all loops should be close to the same size and should hang neatly.

It is best to coil braided line into a figure-of-eight, accomplished by adding the proper amount of twist with your right hand.

For a short rope, 12 to 14″ loops are about right. With a longer rope, such short loops would soon fill your hand to capacity, so make the loops larger.

At times you must coil very long lines, your anchor rode for example. This will be more line than you can conveniently hold in your hand as you coil it.

Hence, coil as much as you can, say 10 large loops, then lay them on deck, coil another 10 and place that on top of the first, building up the coil on deck. Finally, secure that large coil with several pieces of light line.

Another method is to fake the line on deck in overlapping figure-of-eight loops. Now tie the loops with light line, at the

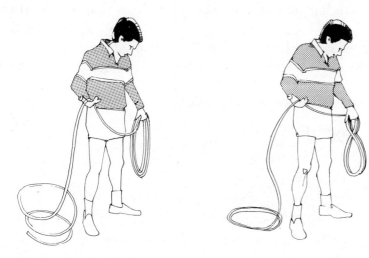

Preferably, three-strand rope is coiled in open loops, whereas braid frequently is coiled in figure-of-eight loops.

207

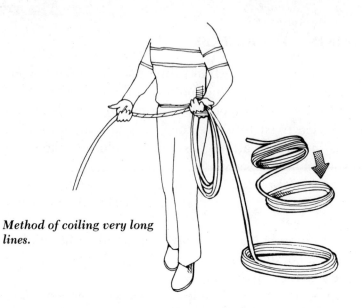

Method of coiling very long lines.

ends and at the center. Then fold in the center. When needed, you merely open out the figure-of-eight, remove the light lines and the rode is ready for use.

Whenever a line must be readied for quick running, e.g., for lowering the anchor on the run, or for heaving, it pays to fake it out on deck in this figure-of-eight fashion, at right angles to the direction of run, or throw.

Avoid all kinks and hockles. The strength of a line is reduced to half if strain is taken while a hockle exists in the line.

Three-strand line has more of a tendency to kink and tangle than braid. Here is a method of clearing a line in preparation for either use or stowage. A line always should be stowed in ready-to-use condition.

Securing a long line for stowage in the locker.

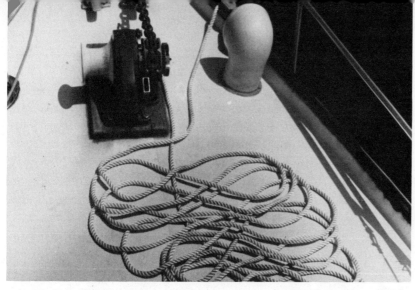

Line faked on deck ready to run.

Starting with one end, coil the line counterclockwise on the deck, letting the kinks fall where they may, in an ever widening coil. When the line has been coiled, pick up the starting end from the center of the coil and re-coil in the proper fashion, in a clockwise direction. Repeat these steps until all the kinks disappear.

Never throw coils of line into a locker without first securing them so they cannot tangle. There are several ways to do this. I find a few turns of the rope tightened around the coil and the end pulled through (where my left hand had held while coiling) serves the purpose for short lines, such as mooring breast lines. For longer lines, pull a loop through

Preparing a mooring line (or sheet) for stowing in the locker.

209

the top of the coil and pass the bight over the head of the coil, then pull tight. In either case, leave a tail (about 12″) for hanging the coil on the lifeline to dry before storing.

A jumble of lines in a locker is poor seamanship. Not only does it look like a donkey's breakfast, but when next you need a line urgently, there may not be time to sort the mess out.

On my own yacht I attached a piece of ½″ dowel just inside the port cockpit locker, about 1½″ from the locker lip next to the cockpit wall. The tail of the longer lines, e.g., foresail sheets, are attached to this dowel with a simple, overhand knot. They can then be removed with one hand. The mooring lines, properly coiled and secured, are laid on a wooden slat floor of the locker. Warm air from the engine circulates and dries all the lines.

Another arrangement is to attach a dowel at the back of the locker fitted with short toggle and eye lines. Because this would require one to get down on his knees and reach away under the side deck, it would not work as conveniently on my yacht but it may be more suitable on yours. Different ships, different long splices!

We no longer need to be concerned with rot in our lines since rope made from natural vegetable fibers, hemp, manila and such, has just about disappeared from the yachting scene.

Sheets hanging just inside the cockpit wall in the port locker of my own yacht. Mooring lines are coiled and lay on the slatted floor of the locker.

210

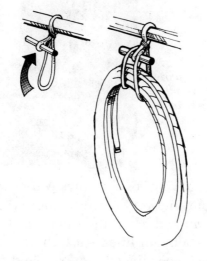

One method of securing commonly used lines for convenience and easy retrieval.

A few problems still need to be considered in order to prolong the life of our lines. Sand, chips of shell or rust, imbedded in the line can cause serious internal abrasion. Whenever possible, hang up the line and hose it down with freshwater. Don't stow your lines under a pile of rusty chain or anchor, and don't stow them near your exhaust pipes.

Sunshine will cause all synthetic lines to deteriorate. We cover nylon sails to protect them from the sunlight. The same sunlight damages nylon lines. Don't leave them out any more than necessary.

Abrasion caused by sharp edges on chocks or cleats, rubbing on coral, stones, concrete docks and the like not only will wear away the surface, but can put deep nicks in the line and even cause it to part. This is something to take into account when sizing anchor line or mooring lines. A ¼" cut in a ½" line only reduces the strength by about half. A ¼" cut in a ⅜" line makes it almost worthless.

If you have a permanent berth, it pays to use chain around dock rings, bollards, and anywhere the line is more or less permanently attached. Anti-chafe material always is a good investment as a means of preventing wear. If you're berthed in a region with significant tides, it may be worthwhile to

211

Permanent after spring and quarter breast lines are attached to a piling with chain and shackles to reduce danger of chafe.

slip large rings over pilings you need for docking. By attaching your lines to the rings, not to the pilings, your lines will move up and down the pilings as the tides change with the rings—not your lines—absorbing most of the punishment.

Check your lines frequently and turn them end-for-end as necessary. Do not expect even nylon lines to last forever.

Handling An Auxiliary Under Power

Sailboats, when backing down, exhibit a will of their own. Even going forward, they sometimes are hard to understand and cause many a trauma and near disaster.

Learn early on how your boat handles under power. Usually at moderate speeds (ahead) there is little problem. It is at slow speeds, forward and reverse, and in the act of stopping, that problems arise. A yacht, whether one ton, 10 tons

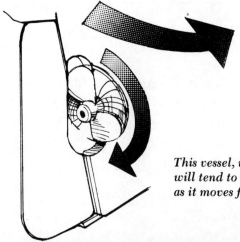

This vessel, with a right-handed prop, will tend to pivot the stern to starboard as it moves forward at low speed.

or 20 tons, will not stop on a dime. The braking force of the engine/prop combination does not behave like the brakes on a car. Let's compare the two for a moment.

A land vehicle follows the direction of the front wheels, whether in forward or reverse, and pivots on them. A boat, however, turns by pivoting about a central point. Steering forward, the bow moves to one side, the stern to the other. The keel, rudder and prop control the boat's maneuverability, and to make it worse, wind and current usually add to the difficulty.

Props are either right-handed or left-handed. When viewed from astern, engine in forward, they turn clockwise or counterclockwise respectively. A boat with a right-handed prop (clockwise) when in forward, kicks its stern to starboard, and at the same time the bow tends to port.

When the prop wash is hitting the rudder, as when the boat is making way forward, the "kick" effect is not large. In fact, at normal speeds it is unimportant. However, when maneuvering at very slow speeds, particularly in reverse, the effect is far greater. Hence it is important to learn which prop you have and how its characteristics can be used to advantage.

Remember a right-handed prop kicks the stern to starboard

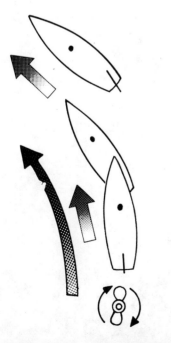

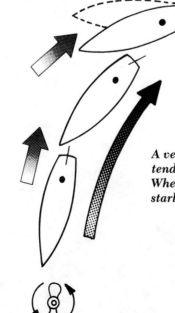

A vessel with a right-handed prop will tend to steer to port when going ahead. When in reverse the bow turns to starboard.

213

in forward, to port in reverse. A left-handed prop kicks the stern to port in forward, to starboard in reverse. The bow is kicked in the opposite direction to the stern.

On a boat with a left-handed prop, it is better to approach the pier starboard side to (all other factors being equal, which they rarely are). When the engine is put in reverse to stop the boat's forward motion, the stern kicks in towards the pier.

The kick effect only is of concern to us in the first moments of applying power. Thus, with short bursts of throttle, forward or reverse, we can effectively control a stationary or slow-moving yacht.

All boats do not behave in the same way and it is wise to practice and learn early in the game how yours behaves.

It is in reverse that you will generally experience the most difficulty, particularly if there is any wind. A sailboat backing down tends to turn its stern into the wind. At times, the only answer is to warp your boat into a better position with lines, or to a kedge out into the channel.

Barring adverse wind and current, you can turn about in very confined quarters using the kicking effect. The boat

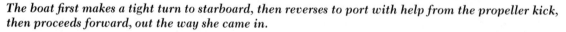

The boat first makes a tight turn to starboard, then reverses to port with help from the propeller kick, then proceeds forward, out the way she came in.

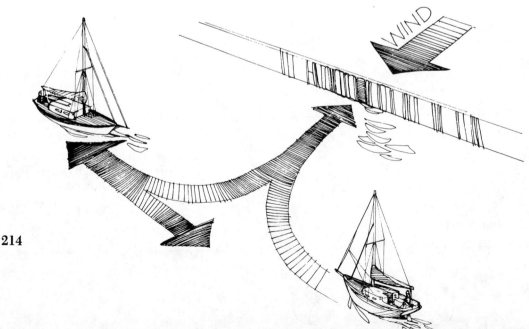

214

with a right-hand prop, which kicks the boat to the left going astern, can turn quickly by leaving the rudder over to starboard while the engine is gently moving ahead *and* astern alternately at low speed. The kick ahead will start the bow paying off and the stern going clockwise, while a kick astern will take the stern and bow around in the same direction while stopping the forward motion.

Every boat will turn more easily in one direction, either clockwise or counterclockwise, depending on the "hand" of the prop.

Practice makes perfect (well, almost) and you eventually will be able to control your boat in reverse.

USING ANCHORS AT DOCKSIDE

Many times you will combine the use of dock lines and one or two anchors.

THE MEDITERRANEAN MOOR

One system, rarely used in North America but common in the Mediterranean, is known, naturally, as the Mediterranean moor. It is getting increased usage wherever both anchoring space and dockside space are limited.

Usually the boats will all line up, sterns tied to the dock with two lines and with one or two anchors secured to the bow and holding each off.

The usual procedure is to drop the hook well out ahead of your selected mooring spot, then to back carefully in between two other yachts, hoping that their crews will have enough respect for their own topsides to guide you and handle fenders.

The first question is whether to go in bow first or stern to. Even if the majority tie up stern to, it may not be wise to follow the crowd. Doing so has the advantage of commonality, if that is an advantage. Perhaps it is easier to get on and

215

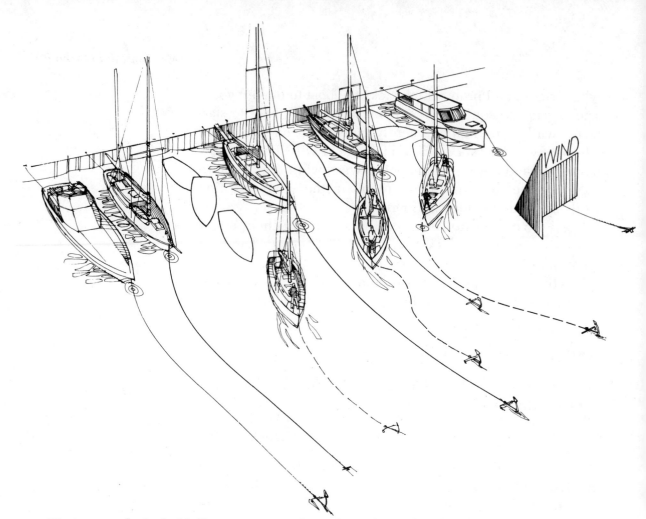

Most commonly, in the Mediterranean moor, the anchor is dropped well away from the wall and the yacht backs down under power, securing to the wall with stern lines. Put out fenders on both sides and station crew members so as to avoid hitting adjacent boats. Considerable backing and jockeying may be required.

off the yacht via a gangplank from the transom. Stern-to docking makes escape easier in event of any emergency.

However, securing bow to has the distinct advantage of much greater privacy. The crowd of dock walkers cannot peer down your hatchway and see all that is going on. The mooring procedure is definitely easier, for you are proceeding ahead and every boat is easier to handle when moving forward than astern. Getting ashore is more difficult—one must climb over the bow pulpit—though many yacht build-

216

ers, particularly European ones, have planned for this by including a gate in the center of the pulpit. Finally, if properly anchored off the stern, getting out in a hurry presents very little problem: Haul in the anchor and go. One last point in favor of mooring bow to; it does not endanger self-steering gear nor transom-hung rudders.

In either case, a heavy anchor, bower or kedge, should be set at least three boat lengths out from your resting place. It is even better to have scope of four to six boat lengths, especially if most of it is chain. Nylon, with its stretch characteristics, is not suitable here for it will not keep you in place as well as chain.

Your anchor should be buoyed and permanently marked

Another way to achieve a Mediterranean moor is to approach the dock bow first, attach a line, back out, drop anchor, and then pull the boat back to the dock.

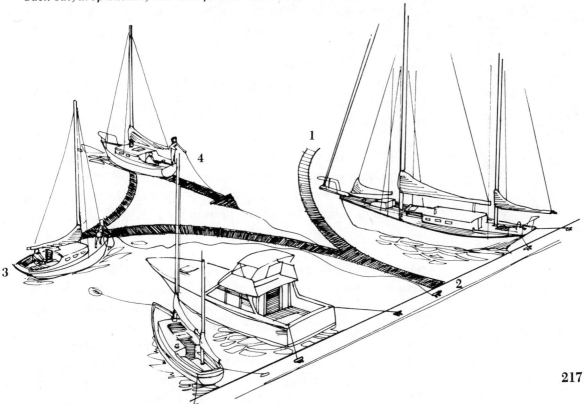

with your yacht's name. Try to avoid anchoring too near other anchors.

Very few yachts have any form of roller, windlass or chain locker for handling ground tackle off the stern. Lacking these features you are faced with the problem of protecting the deck-edge aft, and usually this means handholding the line as it pays out. Of course, if you had the foresight to install a roller or other form of protection, that problem is solved.

Chain should be ranged out on deck so it will run freely. Alternately, a heavy-duty plastic bucket can hold the chain, providing it is fed into the bucket carefully so it will feed out again smoothly.

Line should be faked in figure-of-eight style, not coiled. A tangle in the line could turn the whole procedure into a disaster for you, a big joke for all the spectators. Be sure the bitter end is made fast. Setting the anchor essentially is the same as discussed earlier. If it doesn't set securely, try again.

Be sure you have enough rode available, even if you have to lash together a couple of mooring lines. What would you do if you bring the rode up tight, only to find your nose up to the stern of those other yachts? You are not really there to provide amusement for their crews who are watching, ready to assist you, are you?

A few warnings. You must have fenders on both sides. Don't count on those of your neighbors. Be certain your dinghy is out of the way. It is best to have it on deck. But if so, you will not likely be able to launch it easily with other boats tight up against you on both sides.

As in anchoring, arrange signals in advance between skipper and crew. Be sure you all know the plan. Good teamwork between the helm, the ground tackle crew and the crew handling dock lines is very important. Consider, too, if you're abroad, that communication with your neighbors may be difficult. Fortunately, seamanship is the same in all languages.

Another method is to drop your anchor where needed, as before, then take a long line ashore by dinghy, secure it to a dock bollard and return to the yacht.

Then, as you haul in on the line pulling your boat to the dock, you let out your anchor rode, ensuring that the anchor is dug in securely.

This method, or variations of it, is a good one for the singlehander, or when one's engine fails—or if the current and/or wind is broadside to the boats.

THE BALTIC MOOR

Few of us willingly moor alongside a crumbling or tumbledown pier, or moor on the windward side of any dock, barge or whatever. At times we have no choice. At other times the lee side unexpectedly becomes the windward side and we may be found pinned against the dock. Our topsides are taking a beating and we must do something about it.

Setting a breast anchor usually will solve the problem. It can be dropped before you arrive at dockside, preferably with a scope of 3:1 (chain) or 5:1 (rope), or it can be taken out in the dinghy. It not only will keep your boat from banging against the dock, but will permit you to kedge off, away from the dock into safer water, when it comes time to leave.

If there is danger of other boats snagging your rode, bring it under the keel and up on the inside. This will keep it low down in the water, and increase the scope ratio tremendously, although it's likely to take some of the anti-fouling off your keel and hull. That, however, is a modest price to pay in exchange for preventing topsides scars. When it comes time to pull away, this line will have to be transferred to bow, stern or midships outside.

If you attach two lines to the anchor before dropping it, taking one to the bow and the other to the stern, you can control the drift speed and your boat's attitude to the dock merely by paying out the line.

Whatever technique you use, it is wise to buoy the anchor. Debris is always more common at the bottom of harbors.

219

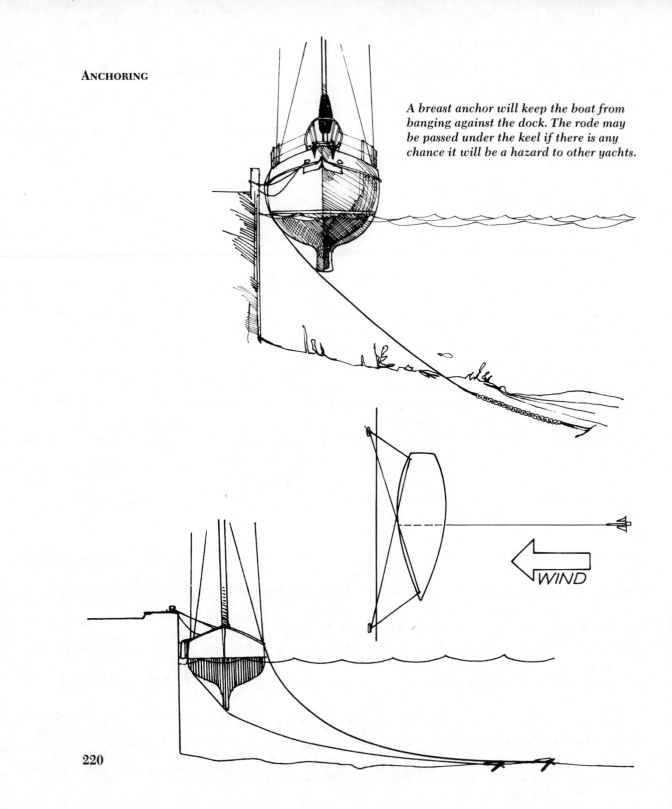

A breast anchor will keep the boat from banging against the dock. The rode may be passed under the keel if there is any chance it will be a hazard to other yachts.

WIND

220

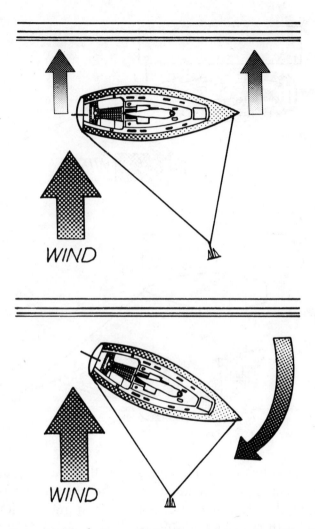

Attaching a spring line between the anchor and stern as well as the rode will help control the direction in which you will drift down to the dock.

You also can use an anchor dropped off the stern with short scope as a means of slowing the boat as you move downwind into a slip or crowded berth. This, as we described earlier, is drudging. However, it is far better to set the anchor where you will have a scope ratio of about 5:1 when you reach your berth and control your speed by the rate at which you pay

221

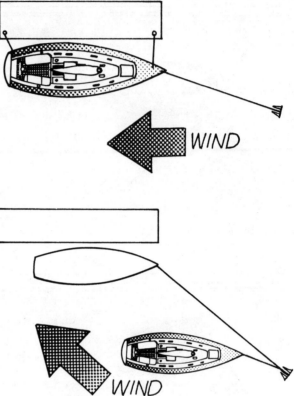

Dropping an anchor well off the dock as you back down into your berth will provide you with means of kedging out to clear water when you're ready to leave.

out line. This has two advantages over the dragging anchor. If you miscalculate and must stop, the set anchor is your insurance. Also, it provides a means of helping you get away from the berth later by kedging out.

PERMANENT MOORINGS

So-called permanent moorings are intended for securing boats that will be left unattended for long periods. Individual yachtsmen rarely design and set their own moorings. Unfortunately, they usually must accept what is offered to them or

222

go somewhere else. We described earlier how to make a mooring with three or more anchors for when you must leave your yacht unattended in some remote harbor.

It is well to know what should be under the mooring buoy, even though you may not personally have an opportunity to inspect it.

Moorings may consist of anything from concrete blocks or even old engine blocks, to mushroom anchors or chain grids stretched across the harbor bottom.

A concrete block may not be a very efficient mooring, but anything heavy enough, sufficiently durable, and thoroughly buried in hard sand, thick mud or clay, will take a great strain. Even heavily creosoted railway ties, well buried, serve quite satisfactorily—until they rot, that is!

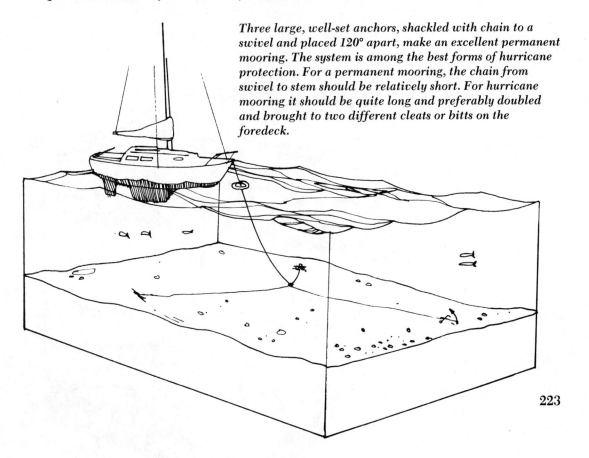

Three large, well-set anchors, shackled with chain to a swivel and placed 120° apart, make an excellent permanent mooring. The system is among the best forms of hurricane protection. For a permanent mooring, the chain from swivel to stem should be relatively short. For hurricane mooring it should be quite long and preferably doubled and brought to two different cleats or bitts on the foredeck.

223

Here's a table for sizing mushroom anchors from an article in the November, 1980, issue of *Cruising World,* written by Katy Burke, N.A. More material appears in *Piloting, Seamanship and Small Boat Handling,* by Chapman, (Hearst Corporation, N.Y.).

Over a long period of time a permanent mooring offers greater security than your boat's own ground tackle.

Boat		Mush-room	Heavy Chain		Light Chain		Pendant (nylon only)	
Displace-ment, lbs.	Length	lbs.	Size	Length	Size	Length	Size	Length
TO: 5,000	TO: 25'	250	¾"	30'	⁵⁄₁₆"		⅞"	
15,000	35'	350	1"	40'	⅜"	Depth of	1"	3 times
35,000	45'	450	1"	50'	⁷⁄₁₆"	water at	1¼"	freeboard
60,000	55'	550	1"	60'	⁹⁄₁₆"	highest tide	1½"	at bow

To determine the size of mushroom anchor and chain, use your boat's displacement rather than its overall length.

A mooring arrangement as described by Katy Burke in Cruising World *magazine.*

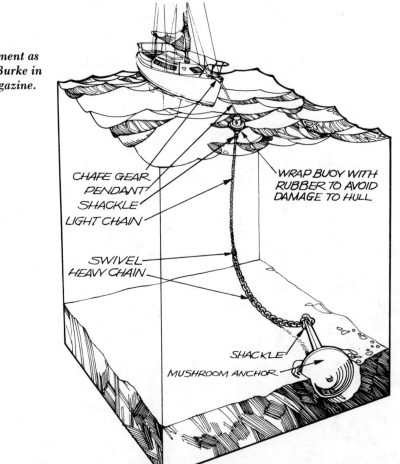

CHAFE GEAR
PENDANT
SHACKLE
LIGHT CHAIN

WRAP BUOY WITH RUBBER TO AVOID DAMAGE TO HULL

SWIVEL
HEAVY CHAIN

SHACKLE
MUSHROOM ANCHOR

The extent to which the mushroom is buried is quite important. A mushroom anchor that is not well buried has no more holding power than an old engine block of comparable weight.

Just as in an anchoring system, the "weak link" factor must be taken into account. Because the mooring will be left in the water for a prolonged period, only the best material should be used, chain, swivels, shackle, seizing wire and so on. It is important to avoid any dissimilar metals, which may cause electrolysis and fast corrosion.

There is no way of knowing how badly the materials have corroded without visual inspection. A diver sometimes can make an inspection. The only safe way, however, is for the owner to raise the mooring every two years and check it visually, inch by inch.

USING UNKNOWN MOORINGS

Whenever you pick up a strange mooring, you must be concerned with its holding power. Don't be deceived by a clean, well maintained float. It is the part under the water, securing the float to the bottom, that you rely on. Until you are certain of its strength, it is wise to set an anchor watch, at least in bad weather.

Try raising the float to deck level to examine part way down the chain. If it is not in good shape and shows signs of wear and corrosion, you may be reasonably certain the lower portion is even worse. Secure the boat to the mooring the same way you secure the boat to its anchor rode.

You may use rope or chain, though chain is very difficult to handle in the average bow chock. If it should jump out of the chock or fairlead in bad weather, it could rip out a pulpit leg or stanchion, or saw through the deck rail. If using rope, include thimbles and seize them well. Shackles should also be seized, and chafe-guard should be placed wherever necessary.

My own boat hung on a mooring for three years in a Chicago harbor some years back. I used two ⅝" nylon rope pennants, each through a chock to one side of the bow fitting and secured to heavy deck cleats. Only once was the boat in danger. In a November storm, one of the chafe-guards was cut through and one rope was severed three-fourths through. In the same storm, at least 12 out of 100 boats either parted their lines and were washed ashore or were sunk at their moorings. To my knowledge, no mooring failed.

PICKING UP A MOORING

Like everything else, capturing a mooring is easy when you know how. A few suggestions may make it easier.

We use a simple system for the benefit of the mate (and the skipper too, for I pick up the mooring singlehanded.) A 6' dan buoy with a flag is attached by about 8' of ¼" line to one of the pennants. The mate can easily reach this from deck level, pull it under the pulpit and get the pennant loop onto a cleat. Then, with the boat tethered, both mooring lines are secured properly, through the fairleads to the cleats.

Picking up a strange mooring buoy is only a little more

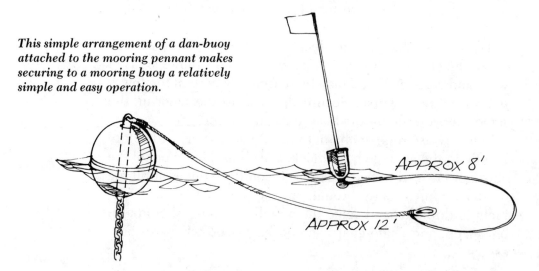

This simple arrangement of a dan-buoy attached to the mooring pennant makes securing to a mooring buoy a relatively simple and easy operation.

APPROX 8'

APPROX 12'

difficult. If mooring pennants are attached a long-handled boathook may do the job. In any kind of a breeze, even a hefty seaman can't hold a mooring with a boathook for more than a few seconds. The foredeck crew must act smartly, and of course, the skipper must bring the boat into the proper position, head to wind, precisely.

A simpler way to put on that initial tethering line is to use a big slip knot or running bowline in a stiff rope, drop it over the whole buoy, lassoing it around the chain underneath.

Then you can take your time to secure better pennants to the ring in the top of the buoy, pull the buoy out of the water and reclaim the lasso.

If under power, approach from dead downwind, heading slowly toward the buoy. The crew on the foredeck should point to the buoy if it is out of the skipper's line of vision, indicating to him how far away it is.

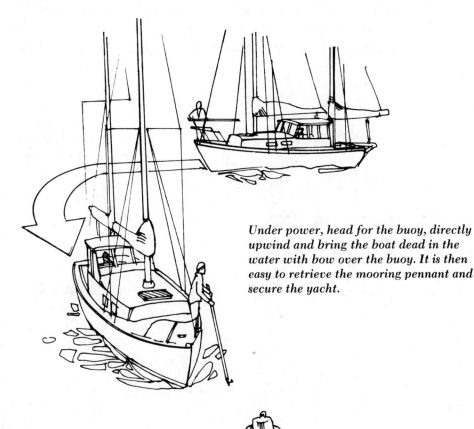

Under power, head for the buoy, directly upwind and bring the boat dead in the water with bow over the buoy. It is then easy to retrieve the mooring pennant and secure the yacht.

At the appropriate moment, the crew indicates "stop" and the skipper puts the engine in neutral. If there is a strong breeze or current the crew must act fast, pick up the pennant and secure it on a cleat or the bitts. Then you can make all fast in a proper and permanent manner at leisure. The important point is to get that line onto a fastening point before the boat drifts down and away.

The dan buoy described earlier is a great help in this operation. If you should miss first time, let go and try again, being very careful not to run over and tangle the pennants in the rudder or prop.

Coming to a mooring buoy under sail is only slightly more difficult but it does require considerable practice.

It's best to use the mainsail only, taking the jib off to provide maximum foredeck working area.

Approach downwind, avoiding other boats moored nearby and turn into the wind with just enough speed to carry her way to the buoy. All boats are different in this respect. Wind, current and waves will affect how much or how little way a

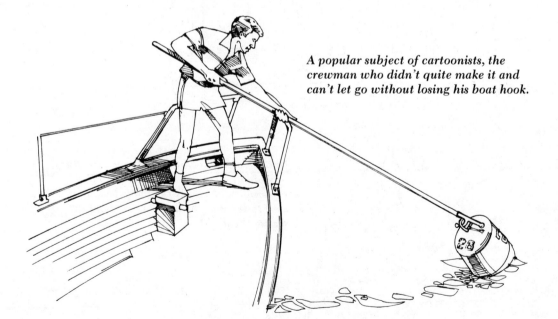

A popular subject of cartoonists, the crewman who didn't quite make it and can't let go without losing his boat hook.

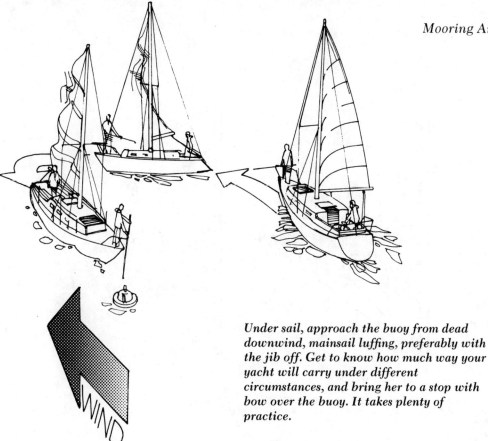

Under sail, approach the buoy from dead downwind, mainsail luffing, preferably with the jib off. Get to know how much way your yacht will carry under different circumstances, and bring her to a stop with bow over the buoy. It takes plenty of practice.

boat will carry. Only practice and good judgment will help you in estimating how far she will carry her way.

Make sure the mainsheet is free and the sail is luffing as you come up to the buoy. Again, the crew must act smartly. If the crew is unable to fasten the pennant instantly, the boat must fall off and sail around and try again. Think this maneuver out ahead of time if the mooring area or anchorage is crowded.

RAFTING AT DOCKSIDE

Many times in our popular, smaller harbors there is no alternative to lying alongside another yacht. At times the rafts will be four or five deep.

229

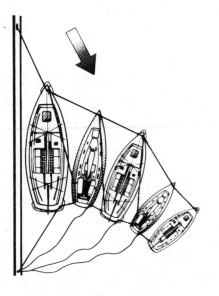
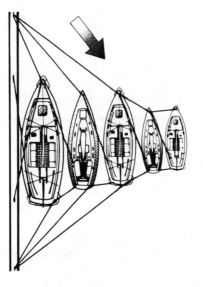
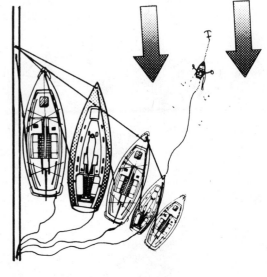

When rafting at dockside, the larger boats lie nearest the dock. Watch for potential danger to spreaders. Outside boats may have to take long lines to the dock or even lay out an anchor, well ahead. Note how much easier it is to leave raft with wind/current than against.

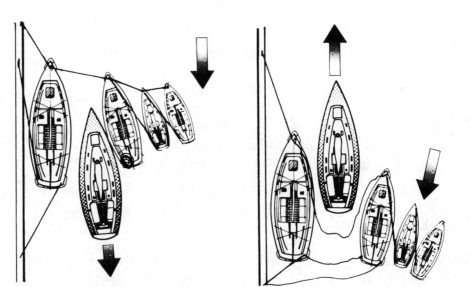

In benign conditions, it is simple to achieve such a raft and the only problem comes with weather change or when someone on the inside wants to leave the raft.

The basic rules for safety, convenience and consideration of others are:

1. The larger yachts should occupy the inside.

2. Use two or more large fenders placed near the wider parts of both hulls. The boat joining the raft uses his fenders. Have a spare handy that can be moved quickly wherever needed.

3. Usually bow and stern breast lines plus fore and aft spring lines are needed. Have all lines ready as you approach the raft.

4. Take particular care to avoid contact between spreaders on adjacent yachts. Sometimes this necessitates alternating bow to stern but this is not practical in a strong breeze or current. In such cases, the yachts must be staggered in order to avoid spreader and rigging damage.

5. If breeze or current is a consideration, lines should be taken out from the boats at the outside of the raft to the dock, as far ahead and behind as conditions permit.

6. Be alert for changes in wind or sea conditions. You may be required to get up in the night to change fenders or even to leave if the seas are causing the boats to bang together with force.

7. Lines taken to bollards on the pier should use large loops brought up from below so that each boat may take off his lines without disturbing the others.

When other lines are already on a bollard or cleat, bring your line up from below before securing. This permits the other to cast off without interference.

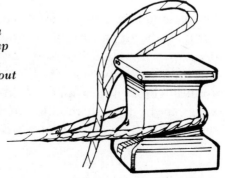

8. It may be necessary for the outside yacht to lay a kedge well upwind or upcurrent, in order to take the strain or even in both directions in a fluctuating tidal stream.

9. It always is good manners to ask "permission to lie alongside" if there is no prearranged plan. Rarely is this refused without good reason.

10. Is it proper to raft to an unoccupied yacht? Personally I don't think it ever proper to raft without permission, except perhaps if there is no alternative. In some tiny anchorages and docks, where space is at a premium, local custom permits —even requires—rafting. If this is the case, permission is not necessary.

11. In close quarters, a great deal of consideration for one's neighbors must be shown. Keep music and loud conversation down. Terminate parties early unless all are included. Avoid running chargers, air conditioners, refrigeration compressors and other noisy machinery as much as possible.

12. Always walk across the foredeck of the yachts between you and the pier. The cockpit is an extension of the living room. Using it as a passageway is an invasion of privacy. Be sure your shoes and those of your guests are clean. Tread softly.

13. Yachts with pets aboard should be particularly careful and should choose the pierside spot whenever possible.

14. Find out what time the yachts on both sides of you plan on leaving. Be on deck with your crew to help, especially if an inside boat is moving out. On the other hand, if you are the outside boat, and getting away early, surely you can manage to do so without disturbing your neighbor.

It is in the departure phase that a fracas so frequently will develop with shouting and frayed tempers. Such can be avoided usually with a bit of forethought and cooperation all around. The simplest method, in a stiff breeze or strong current, may be to wait for the outer boats to take off. Alternatively, in breeze or current from ahead, it usually is best to

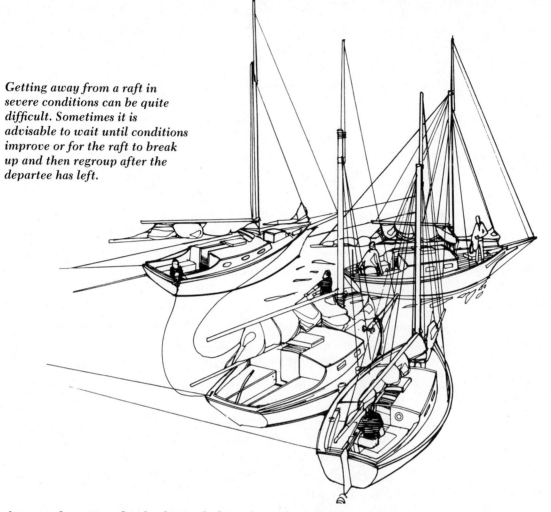

slip out downwind. The boats left in the raft can tighten their lines, rebuild the raft and settle back.

If this is not practical and the departee must go out ahead, real problems can result for the forward lines must be taken off the pier temporarily and a line taken from the bow of the adjacent outside boat, back around the stern of the departee to the bow of the inner one.

The whole procedure must be well planned and executed very carefully. Real problems exist if one or more of the boats is unoccupied. Such are the problems of rafting.

Fortunately, most of the time, everything goes off quite smoothly. The best advice is to use the first method: If conditions are adverse, stay put.

Epilogue

Now that you have studied and digested all this material, consider yourself an expert in the subject. Don't be disappointed, however, if others disagree with you. I mentioned earlier there is little agreement among experts on what is the best anchor, the best rode, or the best techniques.

However, you are now capable of making your own decisions as they pertain to your own particular circumstances. Further, no matter how much you may read, only experience, and lots of it, will really teach you all the intricacies of anchoring, mooring and handling your boat at the dock. Don't ever believe you know it all. One of the pleasures of cruising is there always is more to learn.

Many acts of seamanship must be done instantly and almost automatically. Anchoring, mooring and berthing rarely require such instant actions. Rather, they can usually be undertaken slowly and carefully.

Take your time, think it through thoroughly, discuss it with your crew, before proceeding.

The sea is not gentle. It is not cruel. It is indifferent, though, and unforgiving of overconfidence.

Metric Equivalents

Length Equivalents

1 inch	= 2.54 centimeters
1 foot	= 0.31 meters
1 fathom	= 1.83 meters = 6 feet
1 cable	= 6.08 ft.

1 millimeter	= 0.3937 inches
1 meter	= 39.37 inches
	= 3.28 feet
	= 0.55 fathom

Metric Units

10 millimeters	= 1 centimeter
100 centimeters	= 1 meter
1000 meters	= 1 kilometer

Weight Units

1 ounce	= 28.35 grams
1 pound	= 0.45 kilograms
1 gram	= 0.035 ounces
1 kilogram	= 2.21 pounds
1 metric ton	= 2204.6 pounds
	= 0.98 U.S. tons

Metric Units

10 milligrams	= 1 centigram
100 centigrams	= 1 gram
1000 grams	= 1 kilogram
1000 kilograms	= 1 metric ton

Manufacturers' Addresses

Appreciation is given to those listed here for their help in supplying literature, photos and other assistance.

ANCHORS

Bruce International Ltd.   *Bruce*
Elm Tree House, Elm Tree Road,
Onchan, Isle of Man.

Danforth Div.   *Lightweight &*
Rule Industries Inc.,   *Plow*
Cape Ann Industrial Park
Gloucester, MA 01930

Viking Div.   *Lightweight*
Attwood Corp.,
Box A Lowell, MI 49331

South Western Marine Factors   *Lightweight &*
   Ltd.   *Plow*
P.O. Box 4, 43 Pottery Road,
Poole, Dorset, England.
BH 14 8RE

Sea Spike Anchors Inc.   *Fisherman*
994 Fulton St.
Farmingdale, NY 11735

KB Ultralight Inc.   *Northill*
P.O. Box 14882,
North Palm Beach,
FL 33408.

Sou' West Sails   *Priority*
R.R. #1,
La Have, N.S.
Canada, B0R 1C0

Forges et Laminoirs de Bretagne   *F.O.B. HP*
P.O. Box 141,
29269 Brest Cedex,
France

Viscom International Inc.   *F.O.B. HP*
244 Farms Village Road,
West Simsbury, CT 06092

Charters Marine Inc.   *F.O.B. HP*
80 Ile Bellevue, P.O. Box 22,
St. Anne de Bellevue, Quebec,
Canada H9X 3L4

Sea Grip AB   *Seagrip AB*
Wennerbergsvägen 15,
Sweden

Charters Marine Inc.   *Seagrip AB*
80 Ile Bellevue, P.O. Box 22,
St. Anne de Bellevue, Quebec,
Canada H9X 3L4

Canor Plarex   *SAV*
4200 W 23rd Ave.,
Seattle, WA 98199

Sea Anchors Ltd.   *Stowaway*
P.O. Box 1029,   *Fisherman*
Albany, GA 31702

Paul E. Luke Inc.   *Fisherman*
East Boothbay, ME 04544

Beagle Marine Services   *Fisherman*
Christian Hill,
Colraine, MA 01340

Simpson Lawrence   *CQR Plow*
218-228 Edmiston Drive,
Glasgow, Scotland,
G51 2YT

J. Stuart Haft   *CQR Plow*
Box 11210
Bradenton, FL 33507

WINDLASS GEAR
Ideal Windlass Co.   Goiot S.A.
5810 Post Rd. P.O. Box 430,   27 rue Gabriel-Goudy,
East Greenwich, RI 02818   44062 Nantes Cedex, France.   **237**

Hydra Cap Systems Inc.
26 Alderwood
Irvine, CA 92714

Simpson Lawrence
218-228 Edmiston Drive,
Glasgow, Scotland,
G51 2YT

Goiot U.S. Inc.
3641 Heven Ave.,
Menlo Park, CA

Impex Nautique
187 Place d'Youville,
Montreal, Quebec, Canada
H2Y 2B2

CHAIN AND ACCESSORIES

Campbell Chain Div.
McGraw Edison Co.
3990 East Market St.,
P.O. Box 3056,
York, PA 17402

Dominion Chain Inc.
617 Douro Street,
Stratford, Ontario, Canada
N5A 6V5

ROPE

Marlowe Ropes Ltd.
Haidsham, East Sussex,
England

Imtra Corp.
151 Mystic Ave.,
Medford, MA 02155

MISCELLANEOUS GEAR

Anchoralarm
Populus Products Inc.
14 Scarcliff Gardens,
West Hill, Ontario, Canada
M1E 2A2

Ankarolina AB
Datavagen 51
S-436 00 Askim
Sweden

Geedon Marine Ltd.
Box 11, Colchester,
Essex, England C01 1JY

Harbor Industries
74 Little Harbor,
Guilford, CT 06437

Burt Development Co.
1333 Manor Circle,
Pelham Manor, NY 10803

ADA Leisure Products Inc.
P.O. Box 284,
Ada, MI 49301

INDEX

INDEX